The Wealth and Povei

A wealth of new data has been unearthed in recent years on African economic growth, wages, living standards, and taxes. In *The Wealth and Poverty of African States*, Morten Jerven shows how these findings are transforming our understanding of African economic development. He focuses on the central themes and questions that these state records can answer, tracing the evolution of these African states and the historical footprints they have left behind. By linking the history of the colonial and postcolonial periods, he reveals an aggregate pattern of long-run growth from the late nineteenth century until the 1970s, which gave way to the widespread failure and decline of the 1980s that has been followed by two decades of expansion since the late 1990s. The result is a new framework for understanding the causes of poverty and wealth and the trajectories of economic growth and state development in Africa that straddled the twentieth century.

MORTEN JERVEN is Professor of Development Studies at the Norwegian University of Life Sciences and Visiting Professor in Economic History at Lund University. His previous publications include *Poor Numbers: How We Are Misled by African Development Statistics and What to Do about It* (2013) and *Africa: Why Economists Get It Wrong* (2015).

New Approaches to Economic and Social History

Series editors

Marguerite Dupree (University of Glasgow)
Debin Ma (London School of Economics and Political Science)
Larry Neal (University of Illinois, Urbana-Champaign)

New Approaches to Economic and Social History is an important new textbook series published in association with the Economic History Society. It provides concise but authoritative surveys of major themes and issues in world economic and social history from the post-Roman recovery to the present day. Books in the series are by recognized authorities operating at the cutting edge of their field with an ability to write clearly and succinctly. The series consists principally of single-author works – academically rigorous and groundbreaking – which offer comprehensive, analytical guides at a length and level accessible to advanced school students and undergraduate historians and economists.

A full list of titles published in the series can be found at:
www.cambridge.org/newapproacheseconomicandsocialhistory

The Wealth and Poverty of African States

Economic Growth, Living Standards and Taxation since the Late Nineteenth Century

MORTEN JERVEN

Norwegian University of Life Sciences

Lund University

CAMBRIDGE
UNIVERSITY PRESS

CAMBRIDGE
UNIVERSITY PRESS

University Printing House, Cambridge CB2 8BS, United Kingdom

One Liberty Plaza, 20th Floor, New York, NY 10006, USA

477 Williamstown Road, Port Melbourne, VIC 3207, Australia

314–321, 3rd Floor, Plot 3, Splendor Forum, Jasola District Centre,
New Delhi – 110025, India

103 Penang Road, #05–06/07, Visioncrest Commercial, Singapore 238467

Cambridge University Press is part of the University of Cambridge.

It furthers the University's mission by disseminating knowledge in the pursuit of
education, learning, and research at the highest international levels of excellence.

www.cambridge.org
Information on this title: www.cambridge.org/9781108424592
DOI: 10.1017/9781108341080

© Morten Jerven 2022

First published 2022

A catalogue record for this publication is available from the British Library.

ISBN 978-1-108-42459-2 Hardback
ISBN 978-1-108-44070-7 Paperback

Contents

Figures

Tables

Preface

Avanti economic historians! Thus sounded the call from Patrick Manning in 1987. But instead, the study of the economic history of Africa declined as an academic practice in the years that followed. Studying material change became unfashionable in African history circles, and economists largely confined their studies to the postcolonial period (Manning, 1987; Hopkins, 1986). This has changed recently, and African economic history is experiencing a renaissance (Austin and Broadberry, 2014), with Antony Hopkins, one of the early and central contributors to the subject, describing the surge of literature on material change in African economies as the "new economic history of Africa" (Hopkins, 2009).

According to Hopkins, this new literature originated in North American economics departments and appeared largely unbeknownst to historians. Although Hopkins noted several shortcomings in the historical approach, he invited historians to engage with the research. These seminal articles succeeded in shifting the focus in development economics from associating growth with policy and drawing attention toward the historical causes of wealth and poverty among nations (Acemoğlu and Robinson, 2012; Ray, 2010).

Whether this "new economic history for Africa" is conceptually and methodologically coherent with the "old economic history" of Africa has been hotly debated (Jerven, 2011a). In particular, there was an exchange on whether the new contributions should be called "causal history" (Fenske, 2010b, 2011) or whether the methods result in what Austin called "a compression of history" (Austin, 2008). However, there is no doubt that the seminal papers published more than a decade ago have had an impact on the amount of empirical work that has been undertaken in African economic history in recent times.

The purpose of this short book is to take stock of the many empirical contributions over the past decade. A wealth of new historical data has been unearthed, collated, and organized, much of it from colonial archives but some from other sources such as military files that recorded the heights of soldier recruits and trading companies that recorded prices and wages (Jerven et al., 2012). To date, the new estimates of levels and trends in wages, growth, living standards, and taxes have been presented in a piecemeal fashion. This book takes up the challenge of synthesizing the new knowledge and assessing how this decade of research has challenged and refined the big research questions posed more than a decade ago.

Concurrent with the change in the economic historiography of Africa, the continent has moved from being depicted as the "hopeless continent" to being described as the hopeful continent that is on the rise (Jerven, 2015). In turn, there is an increasing demand for knowledge about the material history of change in Africa. Focus is shifting from explaining chronic growth failure in the so-called bottom billion (Collier, 2007) toward research that can shed light on the role of states in fostering industrial change and that situates the current period of economic growth, or "Africa rising," in the context of the history of economic growth in African economies (Frankema and van Waijenburg, 2018).

One of the central arguments in this monograph is that connecting the colonial period to the postcolonial period fundamentally changes the central narrative in the economic history of twentieth-century Africa. In previous analytical models, the postcolonial period has been treated as an "outcome," and a dismal one at that. Such models identified a historical event in the colonial or the precolonial period as a root cause of this outcome. With the increased availability of time series data, these analytical models need adjusting, since the empirical evidence, on aggregate, tells quite a different story, which is particularly marked in terms of economic growth, and also evident in taxation measures. The aggregate pattern is a long period of expansion, sometimes dating from the 1890s to the 1970s. This gave way to widespread failure and decline in the 1980s, followed by two decades of expansion since the late 1990s. Thus, it seems that the so-called postcolonial growth failure has taken up undue space in explanations of African economic development.

The new description of growth and development since the nineteenth century presented here underlines the need for new analytics. It is no longer enough to explain the causes of the gap between African economies and the rest of the world. A key stepping-stone toward new models of explanation could be distinguishing between the factors that are structural and those that relate economic trends. In his study of poverty in Africa, John Iliffe (1987) spoke of conjunctural and structural causes of poverty. He defined a conjunctural cause of poverty as a sudden change because of discrete events – failed harvests, disease, and so forth. In contrast, structural causes are those that are linked to changes in the political economy, such as property rights regimes or institutions of taxation. While this book goes beyond a longitudinal investigation of poverty, this explanatory framework is also useful for the analysis of trends in economic growth, taxation, and living standards. Research thus far has tended to focus on the gap between low-income and high-income countries, and has not therefore focused on conjunctural and structural causes for these differences and how the differences have evolved over time.

The key contribution is the assessment of what we now know and the certainty with which we know these patterns to be true. To some extent, this contribution and the research that underlies it is descriptive, despite analytical ambitions, but the descriptive material fundamentally changes the tableau of what is known about development in African economies in the twentieth century. The second contribution is that it identifies the relative importance of the types of factors that can explain changes in economic performance and whether these were simple economic conjunctures or we can associate these with structural changes, such as in economic and political institutions. To some extent, this takes us back to the old debates of assessing postcolonial economic performance from the 1960s to the 1990s and thereby returns to gauging the relative importance of internal policy versus external shocks. However, the time perspective here is much longer and I have attempted to take us further toward explaining the patterns of recurrent growth in African economic history (Jerven, 2010b). The availability of longer-term trends on growth, taxes, and living standards allows for comparisons of the political economy of growth in the waves led by external markets in the colonial period, the growth in post-independence states, and the growth in the period after structural adjustment.

Both conceptually and in the source material, this book focuses on states and state records. The book will thus focus on central themes and questions that these state records can answer. It will focus on aggregate economic performance, chiefly economic growth, real wages, and trends in real per capita taxes. Other central themes in African history, such as agrarian change, religious institutions, and gender, are missing in this account. One of the central findings of my previous research (as summarized in Jerven 2013) is that what is visible in the state records across space and time varies. One could perhaps view that as a weakness of the study, but because the book takes as a starting point the idea that the state record is a kind of a fingerprint of the state and its activities, that record can serve as a lens through which we can gauge state activity and state capacity. However, that does not always mean that the growth we see is to be equated directly with "development" in a broader sense.

A general survey text in African economic history has not been published since Austen's 1987 book. The present book is not meant to replace the work of Austen, or that by Hopkins on West Africa (1973). Rather, it is intended to complement them and present new quantitative records based on research on material change in the twentieth century. The book is thematically organized around the big questions of economic growth, living standards, and state formation from the late nineteenth century into the twenty-first century. It takes stock of the amount of empirical work done on material change and African states in the past decades. The challenge is to consider evidence on growth, living standards, and taxes across African countries and link their colonial and postcolonial histories.

Acknowledgments

Complete acknowledgments for this book would require an autobiographical essay that neither space nor the attention of the reader permits. I first sketched an ambitious table of contents in a notebook during a transatlantic flight more than a decade ago, but the research underpinning the book had been underway before I even dreamed of becoming an academic researcher. This book delivers on promises made during the initial research at Simon Fraser University that followed my doctoral thesis in Economic History at the London School of Economics. I am grateful for further funding that allowed me to build on that research on the economic development of African states from the Social Sciences and Humanities Research Council in Canada, and a current grant on the capacity to count and collect from the Swedish Research Council, administered by the Economic History department at Lund University. A list of research assistants who have helped me collect data on taxes, wages, prices, imports, exports, population, and so forth since 2009 would fill several paragraphs, and if the names of all the commentators and colleagues who have offered advice and criticism through seminars, conferences, and informal conversations were also added, there would soon be a short pamphlet.

On a more personal level, I have moved from being a "promising bachelor" to a divorced father of three lovely children. I have moved from Norway to the UK, to Canada, to the US, to France, and then back to Norway again, where I now work at the University of Life Sciences in Ås with an office overseeing the very orchard where I used to climb over the fence after football practice to nick apples more than three decades ago. In Ås, I have found the time and energy to finish the manuscript thanks to the wonderful pastime of managing my family's organic farm, which has fruit, vegetables, chickens, and five cats. In short, it has been a journey.

One of the professional constants on this journey has been the support of my thesis supervisor, Gareth Austin. I have also, as is documented in the preface, had the joy of working closely with my dear friends and colleagues at the African Economic History Network. Academic work tends to be solitary, but this network has created a sense of common purpose. It was Erik Green who founded it, and I was pleased to be a co-founder on the grant application. I thank Mats Olson and Ellen Hillbom for welcoming me as a part of the excellent Economic History department at Lund University. Lund University and the Swedish Research Council has provided the support for the book with the grant for the project "African States and Economic Development in the 20th Century: Capacity to Count and Collect" (2017–05564). I wish to thank my inspiring and supportive colleagues at the Department of International Development and Environmental Studies (NORAGRIC) at the Norwegian University of Life Sciences, where I have been happily working since 2014, and acknowledge the support of the department for the research funding of data collection and the preparation of the manuscript. Rolf Åsmund Hansen has been my research assistant here throughout and is always reliable. Kate Babitt is the best proofreader I know, and she has worked with me since *Poor Numbers*. Many thanks to the series editor Michael Watson at Cambridge University Press, and for the many helpful comments and advice from the three readers of the manuscript.

This book is dedicated to my children and my love Ellen.

Introduction

The book first describes the recent historiography and poses the questions: what is "new" and what is "old" in the economic history of Africa? The first chapter presents the "new African economic history" and summarizes and considers the emerging themes and contributions of the past two decades. Examining the differences in the approaches economists and historians have taken in interpreting social and economic change in the African past, the chapter identifies the central research questions and seeks to bridge the gaps in the methods of these two disciplines. It sets out a potential agenda for African economic history that goes beyond the divide of "causal history" and a "compression of history" (Austin, 2008; Fenske, 2010b) and moves toward the accumulation of more knowledge. A decade of research, particularly using colonial records, has extended the quantitative boundary of investigation and allowed for a richer economic history of the twentieth century in Africa, which has hitherto focused on the persistent negative effect of institutions on economic performance and the persistence of economic failure. The recognition and substantiation of historical economic and institutional change are important, since a dismissal of both economic growth and state formation as failed projects in the twentieth century risks not learning from history: The key is to understand under what circumstances states developed, and under which they did not.

I then turn to the statistical record and reflect on what it means "to see like an African state" in the twentieth century. The statistical record that has been collected, systematized, and synthesized for this book provides a database that challenges existing narratives on African economic development from the nineteenth century into the twentieth. However, the shape of the statistical record itself tells a story. The history of counting and registering people is as old as documented history. It is a central part of a state's effort to govern people and goes hand in hand with taxation. When we look at state-generated statistical records, we are primarily seeing the historical footprint of a state. We see what the state knew about itself and what it cared to find out. We also see what the state wanted others to know about it. In this chapter, I give an overview of the history of census taking in Africa and evaluate the basis of the architecture of knowledge that colonial and postcolonial states have left behind. It is particularly important to clarify what kind of questions state records can answer and where other types of evidence will have to be used. This chapter sets the ground for the empirical analysis presented in the three following chapters. It concludes with a discussion of further research, especially the use of other data sources that will enable researchers to expand "new economic history" beyond the colonial period and the use of the colonial records.

The most important debates center on the question of economic growth, or GDP per capita estimates. Chapter 3 presents and discusses new data and new perspectives on economic growth in Africa. Interest in the economic history of Africa in recent influential economic research has been motivated by the availability of econometric techniques. This methodology has combined evidence from the very recent past (typically GDP per capita today) with evidence that captures some historical event (slave exports, colonial settlers, or geographical variables) to find some root cause of the relative underdevelopment of African economies. This kind of analysis of economic growth in Africa has given the impression that African economics have been stuck in a zero-growth equilibrium for centuries. A longer time perspective makes it clear that growth has recurred in African economies in several periods. The chapter presents new GDP estimates for the colonial period and discusses other historical proxies of GDP growth, such as terms of trade. New data shows that periods of economic growth are not new in Africa, and thus the chapter seeks to place the recent decades of "Africa rising" in historical perspective.

There is of course considerable variation across regions, including pockets of quite strong growth in some places starting in the late 1890s. In some places, that growth lasted well into the 1970s. This puts recent research in a new perspective. The growth literature has been unduly influenced by the so-called lost decades of the 1980s and the 1990s. This ahistorical perspective is worth correcting, particularly because it opens up new research avenues, such as a comparative political economy of growth in the colonial period, in the postcolonial period, and since the 2000s.

How have African states evolved over time? Chapter 4 addresses the prominent and sometimes disappointingly vague debate in the social sciences about the role and persistence of institutions. Studying the fiscal institutions of African states provides an easily observable and measurable way of tracing the evolution of institutions through the precolonial, colonial, and post-independence eras. This chapter tackles the issue by examining the composition of government revenues and the level of tax extraction for all territories in Africa from 1890 to 2010. The chapter builds on a database on government revenues for the entire continent with consistent long time series, thus opening up new lines of inquiry into the evolution of African statehood.

Chapter 4 presents real per capita tax rates for countries across the twentieth century and makes some analytical contributions by proposing typologies of development patterns in taxation. Trends in taxation are not uniform and some countries follow distinct paths. This takes us some way toward distilling what the relevant empirical and theoretical questions are – those that could and should be asked about levels and trends in taxation in African countries across the twentieth century. The chapter presents a general continent-wide trend in taxation (subject to much country variation). We see increases in taxation from the beginning of the nineteenth century through the 1960s and into the 1970s, and then a decrease in the 1980s. There was a marked increase in total revenue from the 1990s into the 2010s (Albers et al., 2019).

There is a long history of poverty in Africa. However, the most influential narrative of African poverty tells a story that takes place over a very short period of time. The history of Africa by numbers as told by the World Bank starts in the 1980s with the first Living Standards Measurement Surveys. The story is also a very narrow one. In general, there is a disconnect between the theoretical and historical underpinnings of how we understand and define poverty in Africa and how it has been quantified in practice. Chapter 5 reviews how particular types of poverty knowledge have gained prominence and thus shaped the historical narrative of poverty in Africa. It summarizes recent work on living standards. New sources on real wages and evidence from anthropometric research allow perspectives on trends and relative levels in living standards back to the 1890s and until today.

This raises the possibility that the narrative of African poverty that was born in the 1980s is a historical anomaly. Such a perspective may also offer a better perspective from which to reach a historical comparative verdict on the more recent "Africa rising" narrative. First, there is nothing phenomenally new about growth in African economies, and second, since evidence of economic growth leading to poverty reduction during the recent period is weak, the period of growth and poverty reduction may compare unfavorably to growth in the 1960s or even to growth in the colonial period.

A few words should be said about the scope and coverage of this book. The book is first and foremost concerned with the big claims about the causes of poverty and wealth in Africa and therefore examines the actual trajectories of economic growth and state development in Africa across the twentieth century. It is also worth noting what this book is not about. It touches only marginally on the topics of agrarian relations and land tenure. It has little to say about religion and gender, and while it certainly raises issues relevant to political history, it has less of a contribution to make in the domains of social and cultural history. It also says little about the precolonial period. Its dominant focus is what new insights we can get from investigating the colonial and postcolonial state records, and the main part of the empirical investigation is based on Anglophone Africa.

In this focus, many other questions are pushed to the sideline. The most obvious here is the lack of focus on the precolonial period (Reid, 2011). The book inherits the lack of attention to the precolonial from the economic literature it is responding to and the research it is summarizing. It is a synthesis of the research by economic historians in the past decade, and the brunt of that work has been focused on decompressing the colonial period. This means that a lot of the new evidence summarized here is from the colonial period. The new insights not only come from unearthing this evidence, but also from connecting it to the postcolonial evidence. That exercise is harder to extend to the precolonial period. With a few notable exceptions, such as anthropometrics, there is a dearth of sources suitable for creating comparable "statistics" for precolonial Africa. This book's focus is shaped by the statistical sources available. This limitation not only applies across time but also across what kind of topics the book gives attention to. For instance, the agricultural sector is not covered in great detail because that sector does not typically figure prominently in state records. Those sources recorded taxes, imports, and exports, but little about agriculture. The bias in the book is that of "seeing like a state," a topic I discuss further in Chapter 2.

The terms "historian" and "economist" are used often in the book. I identify as an economic historian, in the sense that I work as a historian in terms of collecting evidence and evaluate evidence, but the terminology, models, and categories of evidence I use are mainly taken from economics. Thus, it might go without saying that the boundaries of the respective remits of "economists" and "historians" are sometimes blurred in my work. This is similar to what is meant with the contrasting pair of "old" and "new" economic history. "New economic history" is primarily preoccupied with quantification and in particular econometric testing to make causal claims. What I describe here is a meeting point between "old" and "new" economic history, where a challenge made by big causal claims from econometric testing has been met by the vigorous activity of scholars chiefly trained in "old economic history" to collect and create quantitative metrics of different types of development, mainly across the twentieth century, but also from the nineteenth. Thus, the focus here is about the fields where both "new" and "old" economic history have had new things to tell: Growth, taxes, and living standards.[1] The key interest is in how big, bold, causal claims by economists have resulted in a reaction by economic historians to collect more new data, chiefly for the colonial period, and how this in turn has shaped and changed what we know about changes in growth, taxes, and living standards since the late nineteenth century. The path for this book was already laid by the existing literature, in particular the research contributions since the late 1990s. This is a proposal for how some of the new stylized facts in growth, taxation, and living standards in twentieth-century Africa change some of our research questions. The "why is Africa poor?" type of literature has been dominant and has pursued very large but perhaps too reductive questions. The greater availability of times series data now allows us to ask more refined questions about the wealth and poverty of African states in the twentieth century, and answer them.

1 | *A New Economic History for Africa?*

During the last decade, African economic history has been invigorated by new and innovative studies of Africa's long-term development. In 2009, Antony Hopkins used the term "new African economic history" to refer to the work of economists who were offering cross-sectional regressions that sought to explain Africa's relative lack of development. The year before, Gareth Austin (2008) had referred to the new methods and findings as a "compression of history." James Fenske (2010b) took aim at Hopkins and presented the "new" African economic history as fundamentally different, referring to it as "causal history." In response, I searched for a middle ground, acknowledging that there is considerable scope for conflict when the disciplines of history and economics intersect in the study of the African past because "historians" and "economists" differ in the types of questions they are interested in, how evidence is dealt with, and the role of theory and models – or to put it simply: "there are important methodological differences between economists and historians" (Jerven, 2011a: 112).[1]

The early 2000s were clearly a turning point for African economic history. Scholarly production has responded to the heightened academic exchange. So many new students and scholars have joined the field that Austin and Steven Broadberry have announced that African economic history is experiencing a renaissance (Austin and Broadberry, 2014). Many of those joining the field were likely inspired by pressing questions in the economic historiography of Africa. It is also likely that the growing emphasis on history is a response to the challenge of writing the ever-longer history of postcolonial economies and linking that history with the history of the colonial period, often using newly opened archives. However, the prospect of applying quantitative techniques that are more technically sophisticated than those their predecessors used is probably the strongest attraction for new entrants to the field (Jerven et al., 2012).

Both for newcomers to the field and for longer-serving participants, this is perhaps the most exciting time to be working on African economic history since the heady decades of the pioneer generation of the mid-1950s to the early 1980s. In my short academic life, I have felt the radical change. At the first African economic history workshop I attended, which Gareth Austin organized at London School of Economics in 2005, we heard six or seven papers.[2] We started at 2 p.m. and were dining by 7 p.m. and we fitted around one table. In 2016, the then renamed Annual Meetings in African Economic History held in Sussex accepted more than sixty paper proposals to be presented over three days at a conference that had parallel sessions.[3] Newly minted PhD students who specialize in African economic history are entering the job market, and if these new entrants are allowed to teach courses in their specialization and take on the supervision of PhD students, we may witness a decisive change in the subdiscipline of African economic history.

The publication record already indicates that a rebirth is under way, but it is important to note the particular ways the renaissance has manifested itself. The data presented below is based on three bibliometric exercises. The first exercise documents the probable trend. Over the past decade, there was a clear increase in the publication of articles in economic history that deal with African economic history (see Figure 1.1).[4]

Figure 1.1 shows the three-year moving average of publication of articles specifically dealing with African history in three economic history journals since the 1960s. The presence of African economic history in economic history is still marginal. These three journals publish two issues each year with about eight to ten articles in each issue. On average, each journal publishes about one article on African history a year. Thus, about three out of sixty articles are related to Africa (defined in the broadest sense). In the early 1980s, there was a flurry of publications that related specifically to an exchange with Joseph Inikori and others on the structure and profitability of the British African trade (Inikori, 1981). The trend of increase in recent years, after a period of stagnation from the 1980s into the 2000s, is evident.[5] The peak year, 2014, corresponds with the publication of the special issue in the *Economic History Review* that celebrated the renaissance of African economic history (Austin and Broadberry, 2014).

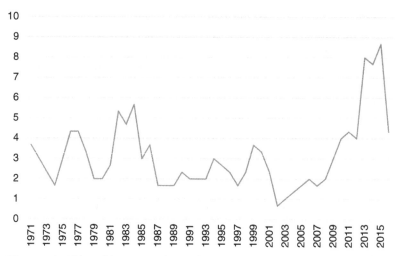

Figure 1.1 African history articles in three economic history journals
The journals surveyed are *Journal of Economic History*, *Economic History Review*, and *Explorations in Economic History*.

A trend can therefore be seen, though not an irreversible one, toward studying Africa in the field of economic history. However, while this trend is clearly detectable in economic history, there is no comparable trend toward economic history in the subdiscipline of African history (see Figure 1.2). This surprised me a little. Before the data exercise, I had expected a broad trend toward more intense study of African economic history across the disciplines of economics, history, and economic history. In retrospect, it makes sense and does indeed seem to substantiate the claim Hopkins has made that the surge in research on African economic history occurred without historians taking much notice (Hopkins, 2009).

The number of articles on African economic history topics peaked at the end of the 1970s and the beginning of the 1980s. This matches claims about a "cultural turn" in history in the 1980s as the study of material change became unfashionable. This was especially true for the study of Africa, where a dismal economic performance in the 1980s turned many scholars away from the topic. It is notable that while the relative decline in the study of African economic history has halted (by necessity, as we were approaching zero publications), there has been no discernible return to the study of African economic history in the

Figure 1.2 Economic history articles in the *Journal of African History*

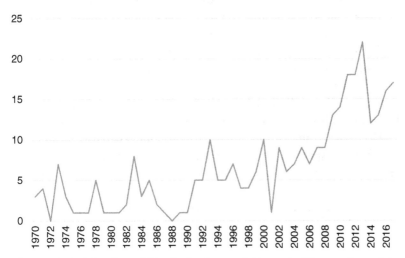

Figure 1.3 Articles about Africa in the *Quarterly Journal of Economics and the American Economic Review*, 1970–2016

Journal of African History, the main outlet for publications on African history. However, today the study of Africa seems to be more in vogue in the field of economics than it was in earlier decades. Indicative of this trend, Figure 1.3 shows the three-year moving average of articles published in the two main economics journals: The *Quarterly Journal of Economics* and the *American Economic Review*. The data record the number of articles that either study an African country or use a global or near-global dataset in which African countries form an important part of the sample.

Between zero and five articles were published per year in the 1970s and 1980s, which then increased to between five and ten articles during the 1990s and the 2000s, and finally exceeded ten for the first time in 2009, when thirteen articles were recorded, and then more than twenty articles in 2013, seemingly settling on a higher plane. The change was largely driven by the shift toward publishing "large N" country studies that examined the effect of a policy intervention on growth rates in the 1990s (e.g., Burnside and Dollar, 2000, which studied the effect of official development assistance on growth) and the shift toward studying the effect of a specific event or institution on the level of income in the 2000s (e.g., Acemoğlu et al., 2001). Because of the vogue of randomized controlled trials that often study the efficacy of certain interventions and often are set in low-income countries, a greater number of publications on development was published in the 2000s in mainstream economic journals, but they did not have a historical angle. (Kremer [2003] is a typical "Africa" paper; it used randomized controlled trials to test the efficacy of different interventions, in this case fertilizers.)

Thus, while we do have a renaissance, the economic history discipline that has been reawakened has taken a particular shape. The surge in African economic history research in economics departments did not necessarily respond to the research methods and questions in ongoing research in African economic history but seems to have been endogenously driven and motivated by technical innovation and data availability in the discipline of economics. The data presented here supports Hopkins's thesis.

"New" and "Old" African Economic History

The chapter now moves to evaluating the challenges the challenges the "new" African economic history has presented and discussing how it fits with "old" economic history. It emphasizes the need for variety in methodologies, conceptualizations, and topics as research proceeds. This synthesis is meant to facilitate intellectual exchanges among the widest possible range of scholars working on sub-Saharan economic history, thereby reducing what Hopkins called "the persistence of imperfections in the market for knowledge" (Hopkins, 1987: 122; see also Hopkins, 1986: 1473; and Jerven et al., 2012) and ultimately promoting new and better-informed projects for future studies.

The mode of inquiry in African economic history has evolved rapidly in recent decades. In 1987, Patrick Manning published his renowned survey of the state of the discipline, where he argued that the need for empirically rigorous, long-term historical perspectives was great for explaining both the present and the past. In policy-making circles, often only a cursory glance toward the economic past has been deemed pertinent to decision making. Economic planners often took post-independence 1960 as the default empirical starting point and neglect Africa's deep economic past. Yet that past is profoundly relevant for understanding long-term development on the continent.

Furthermore, Manning argued, the 1960 date proved to have an imposing presence in the literature on Africa. At the time, Manning identified three literatures: Colonial economic literature, postcolonial economic literature, and economic history. The relatively new but increasingly consolidated discipline of economic history runs parallel to this economic corpus; it spans the precolonial and colonial periods and indeed challenges such divides. Manning argued that economic history could uncover much information that had a bearing on the economic presentism that dominated at the time he wrote.

These different literatures were characterized by different traditions, units of analysis, sources of data, and research methodologies. The post-1960 economic literature, for instance, moved toward the nation-state as the primary unit of analysis, reinforcing the pre-1960 literature, which focused on empire and trade. While economic history has more in common methodologically with what Manning called "colonial economic literature," it differed greatly in perspective, primarily regarding the merits of colonial rule. Against this backdrop, Manning asked how economic history might produce convincing insights about past economic structures and how these insights might be communicated effectively to policy makers. The potential of economic history to speak meaningfully to other disciplines was great. This was especially true of African economic history, which has traditionally been more interdisciplinary than other disciplines and more varied in its influences and intended audiences.

More recent developments, however, have been shaped by the increasing contribution of other disciplines to the study of economic history. Marking the formation of the African Economic History Network, I and my colleagues (Jerven et al., 2012) highlighted the notable resurgence of economic history since Manning's observations. This resurgence has been buoyed by "new" post-independence history that draws upon newly opened archives and by the work of scholars of other disciplines. We specifically noted how Antony Hopkins's (2009) "new" economic history, whereby history is subjected to the key principles of economics, spurred healthy debate about the discipline as a whole, "resuscitating" it from neglect.

I and my colleagues (Jerven et al. 2012: 5) argued that we need to move beyond the obvious methodological divisions and toward a genuinely interdisciplinary approach to economic history. This is both possible and necessary, given that economists and historians ask different questions that lead to different treatments of data and to different modes of theory making. Such differences are not irreconcilable and could be a source of strength. Indeed, interdisciplinary perspectives temper the urge to identify singular, overdetermined root causes of African economic development. Instead of focusing on defining differences, all disciplines with an interest in economic history share similar challenges with aggregating *high-quality*, consistent, and long-run data.

We (Jerven et al., 2012: 7) identify this endeavor as central to the rationale of the African Economic History Network. Members argue that attaining "reliable and valid data" is (and should be) the central concern of African economic scholarship just as much as it is elsewhere in the social sciences. They have audited numerous data sources and metrics and their supporting literatures, from familiar macrolevel indices to those that focus on the individual or the firm. They have also sought to pool assets and remedy gaps by generating data using the same methodology. This will enable economic history to remain empirically grounded while ideally engaging in more theory generation than has characterized the discipline to date. This project was spurred on by the influence of other disciplines and by the growing capacity for and confidence in such an undertaking outside western hubs of influence.

We summarized, as Hopkins did in 2009, the importance of economic history for understanding contemporary economic development: The latter acts as an engine for new and improved work on the former. For Hopkins, recent contributions from economists revitalized a discipline that was seemingly in decline and suffering from a lack of "big arguments" in its defining debates. While historians had arguably focused on more peripheral issues, economists made big questions about poverty and economic development central to their research agendas. Thus, big questions precipitated "big arguments" that economic history, which had lost its "cutting edge," lacked (Hopkins, 2009: 156).

What is the challenge that of a "new African economic history"? It is necessary to clear up what the division between "old" and "new" pursuits in the discipline actually means. Here I provide an explanation for why the "new" economic history appeared and argue that the fundamental reason was internal to the logic of the discipline of economics instead of being prompted by economic events on the continent. Researchers in the discipline entered the "history of Africa" for their own reasons, not necessarily because they were responding to a question a historian had posed, a puzzle from African economic history, or events in Africa at the time.

Rather paradoxically, the discipline of economics was never more preoccupied with explaining why Africa was not growing than when the continent was recording growth rates that were the highest ever seen in history. I also argue that the economists who study long-term outcomes and legacies in Africa remain largely divided from economic historians and historians of Africa. The chapter assesses the knowledge contribution of the different strands of the literature. Ultimately, I seek to map out some of the potential paths for practitioners of both "new" and "old" methods in the history of economic development in Africa. Here, I look for ways to draw on interdisciplinary work to shed new light on old questions and reflect on the inherent difficulties and perils of quantifying economic development in sub-Saharan Africa.

What was the "new African economic history"? Hopkins used the term to refer to new work economists were doing using quantitative methods with the aim of illuminating Africa's long-term development problems (Hopkins, 2009). In particular, Hopkins highlighted the "reversal of fortune" thesis as an explanation for current income differentials[6] and the use of "ethnolinguistic fractionalization" measures to capture weak, perverse, or dysfunctional institutions in sub-Saharan Africa. These had been suggested as arguments and findings that historians and economic historians should and could engage with.

Thus, at first this change in the literature was about eye-catching and controversial innovations in methods. In most cases, suggestions such as the idea that the "slave trade impacted the long-term development of African countries" or that "colonialists tended to work with existing institutions in order to extract resources" or "that sleeping sickness defined economic activities on the continent" were often uncontroversial and even commonsensical statements. While Hopkins (2009) welcomed fresh insights and ideas in the field of economic history, he cautioned that "regression analysis is only as robust as the numerical evidence it draws on" (Hopkins, 2009: 168). Hypotheses that are tested are only as good as the quality of empirical data, which is generally found wanting in the African context. Those who use proxies sometimes base their work on deeply problematic assumptions. One example Hopkins (2009: 166) gives is Daron Acemoğlu, Simon Johnson, and James Robinson's (2002) use of population density and urbanization as proxies for prosperity. Sometimes researchers base techniques such as backward projection on "heroic assumptions" (Hopkins 2009: 168) that are stretched further when they are pushed deeper into the past. Hopkins reminds us that concepts such as ethnicity are "slippery" and difficult to define and, thus, to isolate and measure (2009: 170). The rush to generalize predictably masks contextual nuance and the importance of the particular.

Gareth Austin (2008) had similar reservations about economists' ventures into theorizing about the deeper past. He posed questions about the reliability of quantitative data for all time periods, but particularly for the deep past. More fundamentally, Austin asked questions about the lack of agency this work assigns to Africans, specifically in the reversal of fortune thesis (Austin, 2008: 998). This derives from the perennial assumption that Africans were somehow undone by a mercantile world not of their own making and that global history is determined by the rise of the West over the rest (Hopkins, 2009: 175). The most far-reaching aspect of his critique, however, is his observation that the urge to "compress ... so *much* history" (Austin, 2008: 998, emphasis added) condenses it into binary variables. This tendency occurs both across time periods and between different contexts. The starkest compression of history infers an equivalence between very different types of colonial rule which is at stance with the work of historians and economic historians on the colonial period in Africa (Austin, 2008: 1019).

Despite their detailed misgivings, Austin and Hopkins agree that this new literature must be taken seriously. For Austin (2008: 997), there is merit in examining the prediction of growth theories against the evidence of economic growth in long-term history. Similarly, Hopkins feels that the literature may push historians toward engagement in debates on larger issues and bigger questions (2009: 177). Thus, despite the obvious shortcomings of this literature, Austin and Hopkins agree that it is important.

For Fenske (2010b), however, the methodologies that support big theories are more important than their content. What sets recent developments in economic history apart, therefore, is not the attention-grabbing causal theories of Acemoğlu et al. (2002) and Easterly and Levine (1997) but rather the quantitative, econometric methodologies they use and their carefully crafted assertions of causality. For Fenske, Hopkins's (2009) focus on only two theories and their specificities serves to misrepresent what is truly "new" about economic history (Fenske, 2010b: 179). Fenske emphasizes and discusses the innovative methods of new economic history – regression analysis, fixed effects, instrumental variables, and regression discontinuity – and the various literatures that use them. Such literatures, he argues, are more specific, more nuanced, and more methodologically robust than Hopkins (2009) allows for.

Fenske (2010b) provided a demonstration of the breadth and richness of key econometric literature that was inspired by (but also goes beyond) the reversal of fortune and ethnic fractionalization theses. He countered Hopkins's (2009) critiques of the robustness of these authors' models and the validity of their data. His review of the literature that relies on detailed and robust econometrics concluded that when economic historians enter these growing debates, they must generate both context-specific historiography *and* testable hypotheses that infer causal relationships. He argues that only in this way can they offer research that has both "external validity" and broader "policy relevance" (Fenske, 2010b: 187).

I intervened (Jerven 2011a) in this growing "clash of disciplines" while being mindful of the enduring potential for conflict between economists and historians. I argued that there are important methodological differences between these two camps – in what questions are asked, in how data are treated, and in the role of theorizing (Jerven, 2011a: 112).

I interpreted Fenske (2010b) as claiming that the robustness of a historical argument is "subject only to econometric criteria" (Jerven, 2011a: 113) with the counterclaim that historical evidence is subject to its own methodological criteria, both in terms of criticism of sources and how historians use that evidence in a broader interpretation (Jerven, 2011a). The question must return once again to the quality of data and the painstaking steps historians have taken to generate it in the African context. There are deep conflicts between economists and historians related to epistemology and methodology. Historians generally use the word *evidence* when they talk about their data sources. *Data* suggests truth and historians do not tend to accept that notion. Every data source is biased and incomplete, and thus the word they use is *evidence*, which tends toward treating the data points as individual claims that should be evaluated. Economists, in contrast, approach these individual pieces of evidence as data and use the word *evidence* to refer to the outcome of the statistical tests they have run.

Such differences in assessing the validity of data, however, do not preclude a search for common ground between economists and historians. The work of economic historians falls in between these extremes, and often their role is to navigate these competing arguments about the robustness of data and evidence. Doing so means evaluating the data sources like a historian would, then harmonizing and collating the observations in a dataset that can be used for further analysis. For economic historians, maintaining a good dataset with reliable data is a research output in itself; their focus is not limited to whether their use of a dataset yields statistically significant correlations.[7] There is no absolute rule that can tell us when a wage series is broken or when a series is fine and can be used to tell us something comparable across time and space. The art of the trade of historians and economic historians is making this judgment call.

A dialogue in African economic history cannot ignore the fundamental issue of data quality and data availability. I have suggested that genuinely cross-disciplinary work must start from commensurable assumptions, a process that demands a broadening of robustness checks that go beyond econometrics (Jerven, 2011a: 121). This is not only possible but necessary when forging cross-disciplinary conversations. This conclusion, which echoes those of Austin (2008) and Hopkins (2009), cautiously welcomes the entry of new disciplines, methods, and perspectives, specifically econometrics, to work that seeks to understand African economic history. A focus on causal pathways may indeed provide a fertile ground for cross-disciplinary conversations. The acceptance of these potential new insights, however, is qualified. The somewhat insular conception of robustness of econometrics remains its chief analytical weakness; it circumvents full and frank assessments of data reliability. The key question, therefore, is how to forge core principles that span disciplinary divides.

I think that the controversy partly arose because researchers were ignoring models of explanation, taxonomies, and categories – or simply useful building blocks for stacking and assessing knowledge – that had previously been well established in the subdiscipline of African economic history. A cardinal principle of cross-disciplinary work is that the scholar who is doing the crossing over must make sure that an argument or empirical observation is coherent with the state of knowledge in that discipline. Another key principle is that the person drawing from another discipline must be able to assess what the acceptable data points or conceptual categories are in the second discipline before including knowledge from the second discipline in an explanatory framework.

There are many examples, but a striking one is the surge in the use of George Peter Murdock's *Ethnographic Atlas*, which was published in the late 1960s (Michalopoulos and Papaioannou, 2013). Essentially it is a compilation of coding of societies according to different ethnographers working across different localities at different times. These ethnographical notes of uncertain provenance have been generalized in the atlas so that it can classify societies as "centralized," "matrilineal," or "pastoral," and so forth. The technical usefulness of the data and the robustness of the findings that use this data are questionable (Cogneau and Dupraz, 2014, 2015). More importantly, this data source is anthropological evidence with questionable provenance. When I have confronted present-day anthropologists about the use of this data source, they have referred to it as "a blast from the past" and said that it does not hold up as a credible method or source of data about societies (Jerven, 2011a). Anthropological inquiry has moved on a bit since the nineteenth century, and while categorizing "other" societies was the vogue before World War II, that is not how anthropologists work today. As Austin (2009) notes, using such a source in historical arguments is doubly ahistorical. The observations about institutions in the dataset need to be historicized, not only by dating when the observation was made but also with regard to what is considered acceptable evidence in the discipline of anthropology.

This disciplinary difference between economics and history falls in line with approaches to the usefulness of data points in general. Austin (2009) brought up the point, which Hopkins (2009) reinforced, that the population estimates that Acemoğlu et al. (2002) used to proxy income in localities in the "precolonial period" (or any point from the 1400s through the 1800s) were drawn from an *Atlas of World Population History* that Penguin published in 1978 (McEvedy and Jones, 1978). The intention was not to mock the Penguin atlas but simply to note that population research on precolonial populations has progressed since that date and that a 1978 Penguin publication is not the vanguard of research in historical demography, much like Murdock's *Ethnographic Atlas* is not reflective of current ethnographical methods and categories. Fenske's (2011) response noted the contrast in the approach of the two disciplines to data points with a graph that showed that the error margin in the regression results were not sensitive to increases or reductions in population estimates by as much as even 50 percent.

Fenske's response made the point of miscommunication perfectly. A cardinal point for historians is to get the observations right in their own right, whereas what matters for the economists is whether the observation changes the sign of the coefficient, the confidence interval, or the level of statistical significance. I will return to this point later because I believe it to be a key question for how and whether the communication between economists and historians in the arena of African economic history generates knowledge that points toward new insights. The work summarized in this book is chiefly about improving existing data points or making data points available that do not yet exist. How and why that matters beyond overturning statistical significance tests is a key question.

The disagreement is not only about the validity of data points. It is also about well-established conceptual categories such as making a distinction between "settler" and "peasant" economies in the colonial period. In the postcolonial period, it is normal to make a clear distinction between the countries that were ruled by rural capitalists (such as Jomo Kenyatta in Kenya or Félix Houphouët-Boigny in Cote D'Ivoire) and countries where urban-based socialists had control (such as Kwame Nkrumah in Ghana or Kenneth Kaunda in Zambia). The work of economists who are evaluating the impact of colonialism in Africa is tending toward models that are too aggregative to take into account the knowledge of variations in political systems and in the economic performance of African countries. The first generation regression models on African growth in the 1990s coded all African economies as closed (Sachs and Warner, 1997; Jerven, 2015), and the second generations new regressions on income levels of the 2000s measured all African economies as unproductive (Acemoğlu et al., 2002). The variables used are not sensitive to important variations within the continent. This might be interpreted as the result of not knowing the literature in this field or it might be an omission by design. It is likely a combination of the two, but it follows from the literature that is focused on finding an overall explanation for African poverty that has high enough relevance for all countries, and thus it is too blunt a tool to tease out the finer details. Regression analysis is giving us partial answers to the US\$35,000 per capita GDP difference between Burundi and Belgium as measured today, but is silent on smaller differences over time between Ghana and Ivory Coast. As I have stressed earlier (Jerven, 2015), the regression literature may give broad-brush hints about why Tanzania is not as rich as Japan but tells us nothing about how Tanzania went from US\$500 to US\$1,500 per capita. One partial explanation for this focus is the search for statistical significance and another is the question of data availability, which has had a large impact on structuring the literature.

The end result is that so far work in the "new African economic history" has not been cumulative in at least three ways. I have already discussed the first reason: The new literature did not respond to the old literature but was rather an endogenous innovation in economics. Second, even in the "new" pursuit of African economic history, the literature on long-term outcomes in economics is not focused on rejecting or confirming the arguments of previous work. A great number of papers and articles argue that "institutions" or "history" matter, then when another article finds that yet another variable mattered for outcomes today, it is added to the list as if confirming a grander model that says very generally that "history matters." The result is that one article says that slave exports explain Africa's lack of development and another explains that the prevalence of sleeping sickness was the cause (Nunn, 2008; Alsan, 2015). So far, no one has paused to assess which of the factors appears most important. Instead, the tendency is to conclude that it has been satisfactorily shown that historical events and geographical events can have long-term patterns that are correlated and may be causal (Nunn, 2009). It appears that finding persistent economic effects from historical causes is in itself is interesting.

Third, research has not been cumulative because the literature of African economic history has not primarily been focused on testing to confirm or reject the questions of seminal contributions from literature. In part, this is because economic literature has offered questions and findings that were broad and malleable and have not been strictly testable or because scholars have used the seminal economics literature as a point of departure or as motivation. Also, in large part, the literature that followed seminal contributions from economics has actively rejected its formulation of "why is Africa poor" type questions and has sought to redefine them. To appreciate the importance of questioning the why questions, we need to return to some of the big questions and answers that the econometric literature offered in the early 2000s. I start by presenting an interpretation of how and why African history entered the economics literature.

The Presence of the African Past in the Discipline of Economics

Why did economists come to appreciate the importance of the African past? As I have previously summarized (Jerven 2011a), Jenkins (2006) suggests three reasons. First, the study of economic development is coming of age and is having its own history of failures and successes. Second, economists have long used historical parallels or "stories" to validate development theory. Third, economists associate the discipline of history with using the theory of path dependence to explain economic outcomes. Jenkins (2006: 7) comments that "when faced with studies by economists who use history mainly as a source of data with which to advance unsubtle hypotheses concerning the causes of developmental outcomes, those who had earlier called for scholars to pay more attention to history may regret ever having voiced such a plea, and find themselves revisiting the proverb about being careful what one wishes for."

It is now commonsensical to point to the literature that emphasizes that history and institutions have had a profound impact on African poverty so that even in mainstream economics literature there is an agreement that is not simply economics, but that politics and history plays a big role. Arguments that history conditioned and structured how countries were integrated into the world economy were originally the specialty of radical scholars, mostly those with roots in sociology. Samir Amin, Immanuel Wallerstein, and Walter Rodney formulated such arguments (Wallerstein, 1979). The central argument was that historical events such as the slave trade and the establishment of colonial rule meant that African economies were inserted in the world economy in a way that perpetuated underdevelopment in the periphery.

This interpretation of the causes of economic development conflicted with the mainstream interpretation of the causes of slow growth in African economies in the 1980s. One leading dependency scholar called this a debate between the internalist and externalist accounts of why Africa failed in the 1980s (Arrighi, 2002). The World Bank, a proponent of the internalist account, argued that misguided polices that could be corrected through liberalization were the cause of slow growth (World Bank, 1981). The structural adjustment programs that sub-Saharan countries adopted under the auspices of the World Bank beginning in the 1980s were premised on the policy explanation.[8] The externalist explanation pointed to factors that came from the dependency literature, such as deterioration of terms of trade for primary product producers in the world economy (Toye and Toye, 2003).

Two different interpretations of political economy are at stake that might strike readers as remarkably similar. Both interpretations emphasized how rulers of states were part of the problem rather than the solution. The radical "old" political economy argued that this problem of political leadership was primarily driven by how these states were integrated into the world economy (Amin, 1972).[9] The dependency theory statement of this argument says that while agency clearly rests with Europe in this transformation, African elites played the key role. Such theories focus on the orientation of the domestic political elite. This political economy interpretation argued that in order to break with this pattern, African elites should break ties with the world economy.[10]

In 1981, Robert H. Bates offered a theory that laid the foundations for a new interpretation of political economy. He argued that African politicians chose policies that served their own interests rather than those that favored economic development.[11] The World Bank picked up on the domestic policies that Bates highlighted as growth retarding, including intervening in the pricing of agricultural exports. Instead of letting markets set the price, thus stimulating export growth, African elites set prices low through marketing boards. Bates argued that the reasons elites adopted such growth-retarding policies were that urban centers constituted the political base for many leaders and that they favored a transfer of income from the agriculture sector to dominantly urban-based activities.

This exchange between the old and new political economies, given their different positions on the origins of growth-retarding policies, might have been fruitful. It is certainly true that policies were important. The question was what the origin of elite policy alignments were. Was it the world economy or was it the urban base of many African leaders? Was the behavior of states best explained by their linkage to the former colonial powers or was their behavior determined by the distribution of power in the rural sector? However, such deep diagnostics were abandoned, and a treatment of the symptoms rather than the causes ensued in the form of introducing Structural Adjustment Programs under the auspices of the IMF and the World Bank. Politically, the debate on why Africa was growing slowly in the 1980s and 1990s was settled by introducing the policy reforms of liberalization and privatization that structural adjustment which is commonly referred to as the "Washington Consensus" (Jerven 2015).

The policy changes of the 1980s coincided with a change in academic inquiry. The literature that investigated change in African economies underwent a clear paradigm shift in that decade. The change in how economic development and growth was debated in the scholarly domain brought about great interest in empirical tests of growth theory. This shift began in the early 1980s and came to full bloom in the 1990s (Jerven, 2011a). In addition, several African economic historians who did not embrace dependency theory remarked that they considered the history before the 1960s to be irrelevant, which was a major problem for the World Bank and IMF diagnosis (Hopkins, 1986; Manning, 1987).

This type of investigation was made possible by the availability of the global datasets on economic growth, such as the Penn World Table, the arrival of which was considered to be "an important statistical event" that expanded the boundaries of empirical research (Stern, 1989: 600).[12] The combination of a new methodology and new data sources spurred a great amount of research. The articles and essays this research generated used the methodology of cross-country growth regressions in which the dependent variable was the average growth rate of per capita GDP. The starting point is arguably a 1991 article by Robert J. Barro. His essay exploring the causes of economic growth in a global sample of countries provided the template for the next decade of research.[13]

Barro's model used cross-country regressions with global datasets on growth in GDP per capita and looked for correlations with other variables such as educational attainment, number of assassinations, and black-market currency rates. When he had checked and controlled for many different variables, one central finding remained. There was a large and significant "dummy variable" for the African continent. A dummy variable takes the value 1 or 0; in this case it took the value 1 if the country was situated on the African continent and 0 if it was not. In the regressions, the dummy variable remained significant. Barro's interpretation of the dummy was that the analysis had not yet fully captured the characteristics of a "typical" African country (Barro, 1991: 437). This initiated what I have called "the quest for the African dummy" (Jerven, 2011b; see also Englebert, 2000b).

Following Barro's seminal publication, a literature developed that sought to identify the global determinants of growth. A scholarly search for the right variables began, and while many correlates with slow growth were found over the course of a decade of research, the African dummy variable proved resistant to removal.

As I have argued elsewhere (Jerven, 2015), although the quest did not yield much useful information, it was highly influential. Steven Durlauf and colleagues referred to this scholarly production as a "growth regression industry" (Durlauf et al., 2005: 599). As early as 1998, Pritchett observed that the growth experience of most developing countries was characterized by instability rather than stable growth and warned that the exploding economic growth literature was unlikely to be useful. The general growth regression literature has been described as disappointing. One assessment concluded that the "current state of the understanding about causes of economic growth is fairly poor" and that "we are in a weak position to explain why some countries have experienced economic growth and others not" (Kenny and Williams, 2001: 15).

I made this point quite forcefully in *Africa: Why Economists Get It Wrong* (2015). When the editors of the journal *Development Policy Review* called for a debate, I wrote a short version of my argument with the title "The failure of economists to explain growth in African economies" (Jerven 2016c). Economists Jonathan Temple (2016), Denis Cogneau (2016b), and Dietrich Vollrath (2016) each wrote a response and I was given a chance to offer a final comment (Jerven 2016a). The debate was quite illuminating, particularly as Temple was one of the many scholars who has contributed directly to the cross-country growth regression literature. While he did not write off the research as useless, he conceded that the periods of growth in Africa were under-researched.

Vollrath and Cogneau, who have no particular stake in the cross-country regression literature, were far more willing to cede ground. Vollrath's (2016: 908) position was particularly illuminating: "It is fair to claim that this literature became too enamored of econometric technique, at the cost of ignoring the issues underlying the data that was passed around and used repeatedly. There is definitely a false sense of accuracy given by regressions using this data." He did not contest the claim that the literature had influence in policy circles but argued that the influence of the cross-country growth regressions had waned and that the literature had matured:

One of those conclusions is that research on policy and institutions has taken up too much space in this literature, and that it has exerted an outsized influence on broader discussions of development in the policy world and academia. I do not have tight ties with the policy world, so it is hard for me to disagree with Jerven's conclusion there. But I am closely engaged with academic research in growth and development, and here I will disagree. In my capacity as referee, editor, and discussant across various outlets, the number of papers that I see relying on cross-country regressions to make their point has diminished to nearly zero. Nathan Nunn's (2008) work on the effects of the African slave trade is perhaps the last to "get away" with using cross-country empirics exclusively. (Vollrath, 2016: 908)

Thus, for different kinds of reasons one could argue that the literature of the 1990s was misguided. Yet I think it had a key influence in two areas. The first was that the literature provided a post-hoc affirmation that the World Bank and IMF policy-based diagnosis of the slow growth in the 1980s was largely correct. The second, largely unintended, influence was the idea that African economies were captured in a chronic failure of growth; this became an accepted stylized fact in economics.

The outcome of what I have called the first generation of growth literature was principally that it tended to confirm that there was correlation between the observed average slow growth in African economies and other variables that were supposed to capture "growth-retarding policies," principally state interventions in markets (although there are severe gaps in this interpretation, see Jerven, 2011b). This is what the World Bank reports of the 1980s accepted and it is what provided the justification for policy interventions to liberalize African economies. The key variables were black-market premiums, budget deficits, and other, more constructed variables such as "openness" or "governance."

As I have argued elsewhere (Jerven, 2015), crucial mistakes were made in specifying both the dependent and the independent variables in this work. It is true that *on average* African economies grew more slowly than other economies from the 1960s until the mid-1990s, but that is true only if you take the average of that whole period and let it end in the mid-1990s. It is not true that African economies grew more slowly on average in the 1950s, the 1960s, the 1970s, and the 2000s. They grew much more slowly than the rest of the world in the 1980s and in most of the 1990s.[14] Thus, looking for a correlate of the *average* is misleading in the sense that the research did not explicitly ask what could account for growth in the 1960s, the 1970s, and the 2000s, but took it as given that the average shortfall in growth is what was relevant.

The mistakes that were made in the formulations of the dependent variables are equally important. There were three kinds. The first was the idea that almost all of the variables were endogenous: They were things that could be both cause and effect. Examples include budget deficits and black-market premiums for foreign currency; both might very well be the outcome of slow growth or economic shocks. This was compounded by the second type of mistake, which was the fact that variables such as black-market premium rates for foreign currency were entered as averages, but those averages were directly inflated by the very high deficits or premiums observed in the 1980s. The third mistake was the idea that data such as a perception of corruption or other type of subjective survey data intended to capture "bad governance" were actually observations from the late 1980s and were thus quite literally effects of the slow growth (or rather the negative economic shocks) of the late 1970s and early 1980s.

As I have previously argued (Jerven, 2015), many scholars recognized and noted these weaknesses. There was a distinct trend of decreasing humility about the findings, though. One early article noted the correlation between corruption and slow growth yet concluded that one had to remain agnostic about the direction of causation (Mauro, 1995). Later work noted the correlations between slow growth and good governance with much higher confidence about the direction of causation (Collier and Gunning, 1999a, 1999b).

Yet the doubt about the causality remained, and as Vollrath implied, very few of those articles would have been published today. A second generation of growth literature began in the 2000s that is recognizable by the use of the instrumental variables. One important motive for using historical variables is technical: To use instrumental variables to take care of the endogeneity problem that arises when factors that are supposed to affect a particular outcome depend themselves on that outcome. This was exactly the difficulty scholars encountered who were attempting to quantify the effect of aid, infrastructure, and corruption on development. The seminal contribution of Acemoğlu et al. (2001) was to use European settler mortality rates as an instrumental variable for risk of capital expropriation.

Before explaining what Acemoğlu et al. did, we need to explain the concept of an "instrumental variable." If you wanted to measure the effect of police on crime, you would instantly run into the problem of reverse causality. While police may plausibly reduce crime, crime increases the number of police so that if there are more police in one area, there is probably more crime there too. Recent events in the US do however show that police might also be the instigators and creators of crime, so the correlates of crime and police are hard to interpret. A clever way of solving this kind of puzzle is to add a variable that is unrelated to crime but is related to the number of police out on the streets. Weather could be such a variable. Hypothetically, if it is sunny, there might be more police on the streets. In a regression framework, one could therefore use the effect of weather on police, insert that variation in the second equation, and then measure this instrumental variable effect on crime. The innovation in the economic literature was to use an instrumental variable in the search for a clean causal identification of something that explains "why Africa is poor" (Deaton, 2010). The quest changed from finding a correlate with slow growth toward finding an "exogenous variable" that could explain variation in economic performance but that could not be used to explain the inverse relationship.

The most obvious examples are usually some kind of geographical variable. It is very seldom that political and social systems cause short-term observable effects in geography, but very often natural conditions shape our behavior. So for instance, one of the earliest and most frequently used instrumental variables is distance to the equator. The argument is pretty simple. There is a correlation between average slow growth (between the 1960s and the 1990s) or low income (per capita today) and distance to the equator: The closer a country is to the equator, the poorer it is. It is close to impossible to argue that slow growth in the 1970s caused a country to get closer to the equator. Thus, the argument for the use of instrumental variables goes, the distance to the equator can be used as an intervening variable for anything that correlates with it, and then in the second stage of the equation one can use the coefficient to run the second regression, where you would see the familiar suspects from the first generation of growth regressions, in particular the metrics of "good governance" and "quality of institutions" that grew in importance and frequency of use beginning in the late 1990s.

However, an instrument that is geographical tends to reinforce a narrative that courts geographical determinism and limits the role of politics, society, and economics, which is not the kind of explanation that economists and political scientists would favor. Thus, the time was ripe for a quantifiable explanation that could take a starting point in a historical or political settlement.

On cue, Acemoğlu et al. revived debates about the historical determinants of economic growth with their two controversial theses: The "reversal of fortune" (2002) and the "colonial origins of comparative development" (2001). The former argues that the non-European areas of the world that were the poorest 500 years ago are now among the richest and that the formerly richest areas are now among the poorest. Thus, the last 500 years of economic development constitute a reversal of fortunes in non-European areas. Acemoğlu and colleagues argued that this reversal is explained by European colonization. In the poorer areas, Europeans settled in great numbers and invested in the creation of costly but "good" institutions in the colonies. The second thesis, which built on the first, explained the current comparative development levels in the non-European world using an instrumental variable approach. Acemoğlu and colleagues argued that the mortality rate of European settlers determined the numbers of settlers the colony attracted: Fewer Europeans settled where mortality rates for Europeans were high. This, in turn, determined the quality of the institutions that settlers built in the colony.[15] The argument distinguishes between colonies where extractive institutions were introduced and colonies where productive institutions were established; the latter are the rich African nations today.

These two interventions by Acemoğlu et al. (2001, 2002) were as seminal as the Barro's article had been a decade earlier (1991). In their assessment of the first generation of growth literature, Durlauf, et al. (2005) reported that 145 explanatory variables had been found to be statistically significant and that forty-three conceptually different "theories" of growth had been "proven" in the literature, a result of what they call a "growth regression industry" as researchers added plausibly relevant variables to the baseline Solow specification (599, 639). The second generation quickly accumulated an equal number of variables and theories.

In preparing this book, I made a similar list of the second generation of the growth literature. I am aware that there is a recent review of the econometric literature on the African past (Michalopoulos and Papaioannou, 2019), which is a helpful addition and update to Fenske's (2010a) review, and do not therefore want to recount the arguments in that literature at length here, but in Table 1.1 I have compiled a perhaps representative list of publications that make a "history matters" argument using macro – usually cross-country – evidence, in which Africa plays a central role in the sample.

Most work in this group follows the same recipe: A dataset that has sufficient cross-national variation in a historical or geographical variable that is correlated with an intervening variable such as "institutions" is again correlated with a present-day outcome, such as GDP per capita. The list in Table 1.1 is not complete, but it does

Table 1.1 *Economic literature since 2000 that uses a historical argument to explain slow growth in Africa*

Independent Variable	Intervening Variable	Dependent Variable	Data Period	Author/Year	Title
Artificial borders/straight borders	Ethnic splitting	GDP per capita	n/a	Alesina et al. (2006)	Artificial states
Banning of polygyny		GDP per capita		Tertilt (2005)	Polygyny, fertility, and savings
Colonial-era education	Colonial human capital	GDP per capita	1945–1950	Bolt and Bezemer (2009)	Understanding long-run African growth: Colonial institutions or colonial education?
Colonial governors' pay	Institutional quality	GDP per capita	Late 19th century	Jones (2013)	History matters: New evidence on the long run impact of colonial rule on institutions
Competitive multiparty and "founding" elections	Economic and political reform	Growth per capita	1980–1995	Block et al. (2003)	Multiparty competition, founding elections and political business cycles in Africa
Democracy	Human capital; government consumption and physical capital accumulation	Growth per capita	1970–1989	Tavares and Wacziarg (2001)	How democracy affects growth
Education (various channels)	Education equality	Income inequality (income/GDP)	1890–2010	Van Leeuwen et al. (2012)	Education as a driver of income inequality in twentieth-century Africa

Table 1.1 (*cont.*)

Independent Variable	Intervening Variable	Dependent Variable	Data Period	Author/Year	Title
Effects of extractive policies	Colonial heritage	Growth per capita	Colonial time	Price (2003)	Economic growth in a cross-section of nonindustrial countries: Does colonial heritage matter for Africa?
Ethnic fragmentation	Public policies	Growth per capita	n/a	Easterly and Levine (1997)	Africa's growth tragedy: Policies and ethnic divisions
Foreign aid	Policies	GDP growth & policy change	1970–1993	Burnside and Dollar (1997)	Aid, policies, and growth
Geographic characteristics of trade	Trade	Income/GDP	1985	Frankel and Romer (1999)	Does trade cause growth?
Geography; demography	–	GDP growth/GDP per capita	1820–1992	Bloom et al. (1998)	Geography, demography, and economic growth in Africa
Historical conflict	Postcolonial conflict; national unity/identity	GDP per capita	1400–1700	Besley and Reynal-Querol (2014)	The legacy of historical conflict: Evidence from Africa
Indigenous slavery	Capability and accountability of African states	GDP per capita	1850–1950	Bezemer et al. (2014)	Slavery, statehood, and economic development in sub-Saharan Africa
Length of colonization; level of education	–	Growth per capita	1961–1990	Grier (1999)	Colonial legacies and economic growth
Level of education under different colonial powers	–	GDP per capita and life expectancy		Cogneau (2003)	Colonisation, school, and development in Africa: An empirical analysis

Long-standing experience of a "national state"	–	GDP; economic growth; political stability.	1–1950	Bockstette et al. (2002)	States and markets: The advantage of an early start
Malaria risk; share of population in temperate ecozones	Ecological conditions	GDP per capita	n/a	Sachs (2003)	Institutions don't rule: Direct effects of geography on per capita income
Metropolitan ruler; degree of economic penetration	Colonization	GDP per capita	n/a	Bertocchi and Canova (2002)	Did colonization matter for growth? An empirical exploration into the historical causes of Africa's underdevelopment
Mosquito vectors	Malaria	Growth per capita	1965–1990	Gallup and Sachs (2001)	The economic burden of malaria
Neopatrimonial policies (due to lack of legitimate history)	Colonial institutions	Growth per capita	n/a	Englebert (2000a)	Pre-colonial institutions, post-colonial states, and economic development in tropical Africa
Number of colonial administrators relative to the African population	Colonial institutions	GDP per capita	1920–1950	Richens (2009)	The economic legacies of the "thin white line": Indirect rule and the comparative development of sub-Saharan Africa
Point-source natural resource economies (oil, minerals, and plantation crops)	Governance indicators	GDP per capita	1985	Isham et al. (2005)	The varieties of resource experience: Natural resource export structures

Table 1.1 (*cont.*)

Independent Variable	Intervening Variable	Dependent Variable	Data Period	Author/Year	Title
					and the political economy of economic growth
Political/civil liberties; political instability; property rights	Institutions	GDP growth	1820–2010; 1849–2010	Akpalu et al. (2017)	Evolution of institutions in Ghana and implications for economic growth
Politically relevant ethnic groups	Ethnic diversity	Growth per capita	Early 1960s	Posner (2004)	Measuring ethnic fractionalization in Africa
Polity IV index scores	Democracy	GDP per capita	1955–2007	Bates et al. (2012)	The state of democracy in sub-Saharan Africa
Precolonial political complexity	–	Contemporary economic performance	n/a	Michalopoulos and Papaioannou (2013)	Pre-colonial ethnic institutions and contemporary African development
Property-rights institutions	–	GDP, investments and financial development	1500–1900	Acemoğlu and Johnson (2005)	Unbundling institutions
Savings	–	GDP	1850–1909	Greyling and Verhoef (2017)	Savings and economic growth: A historical analysis of the Cape Colony economy, 1850–1909
Settler mortality and mean temperature	Geography	GDP per capita	n/a	Assenova and Regele (2017)	Revisiting the effect of colonial institutions on comparative economic development

Explanatory variable	Channel	Outcome	Period	Reference	Title
Settler mortality; risk of expropriation	Colonial institutions	GDP per capita	1604–1848; 1985–1995	Olsson (2004)	Unbundling ex-colonies: A comment on Acemoğlu, Johnson, and Robinson, 2001
Settler mortality; risk of expropriation	Current institutions	GDP per capita	1604–1848; 1985–1995	Acemoğlu et al. (2001)	The colonial origins of comparative development: An empirical investigation
Slave trade	–	GDP per capita	1400–1900	Nunn (2008)	The long-term effects of Africa's slave trades
Slave trade	Cultural norms, beliefs, values	Level of trust	n/a	Nunn and Wantchekon (2011)	The slave trade and the origins of mistrust in Africa
Split ethnic groups (between countries)	Colonial border design	Political violence; economic performance	n/a	Michalopoulos and Papaioannou (2016)	The long-run effects of the scramble for Africa
State legitimacy	Policy choices	Growth per capita	1960–1992	Englebert (2000b)	Solving the mystery of the Africa dummy
Taxation and revenue	Fiscal capacity	GDP per capita	1850–2010	Andersson (2017)	Long-term dynamics of the state in Francophone West Africa: Fiscal capacity pathways 1850–2010
Technology adoption in 1500 CE	Technology level today	GDP per capita	1000 BCE–1500 CE	Comin et al. (2010)	Was the wealth of nations determined in 1000 BC?
Terrain ruggedness	Slave-trade history	GDP per capita	1950–2000	Nunn and Puga (2012)	Ruggedness: The blessing of bad geography in Africa

Table 1.1 (*cont.*)

Independent Variable	Intervening Variable	Dependent Variable	Data Period	Author/Year	Title
Trade openness	–	Growth of GDP per capita	1948–1991	Sachs and Warner (1995)	Economic reform and the process of global integration
Tsetse fly	Precolonial political centralization	GDP/economic performance	n/a	Alsan (2015)	The effect of the tsetse fly on African development
Variation in migratory distance from the cradle of humankind	Genetic diversity	GDP per capita	n/a	Ashraf and Galor (2011)	The "Out of Africa" hypothesis, human genetic diversity, and comparative economic development

indicate that we are approaching fifty or so various theories that have been found to have empirical support. The number of potential instrumental variables might soon dry up and we may have already reached the limit of insights from the instrumental variable approach. A number of scholars have pointed out that because of the stringent identification strategies, we select away big important questions that cannot be settled econometrically (Deaton, 2010). The literature is also criticized from within. Just as cross-country correlations seemed like the gold standard for determining causality in the 1990s before becoming outdated in the 2000s, the "persistence literature" has encountered some serious criticism recently. Kelly (2019), who has tested twenty-eight of the most famous publications in this literature, argues that their significance levels might have been misinterpreted because of autocorrelation. He finds when these publications are subjected to tests for this, two-thirds of them fail, and that the regressions are simply making spatial noise fit the analysis. Kelly restates Tobler's First Law of Geography: "Everything is related to everything else, but near things are more related than distant things." Spatial data, in other words, tend to be autocorrelated. Kelly explains:

Take some towns dotted across a landscape and represent their average income levels as elevation on a map. If there is little correlation between neighbours, rich will border poor, leading to a jagged topography. However, as Tobler observed, usually the correlation is long range so affluent places are surrounded by other affluent ones, leading to a gently rolling landscape. Now take some other unrelated variable from the past, say trials for heresy in the middle ages. Again neighbour will resemble neighbour, leading to another rolling landscape. If we regress these variables on one another, peaks in one landscape will often tend either to correspond to peaks in the other, giving positive t statistics, or to hollows leading to negative ones. When the towns cluster together in a few geographical areas the probability of coincidence will be corresponding[ly] greater. (Kelly, 2019: 3)

For a number of reasons then, there is a need to decompress history and to focus on historical change and investigate more granular research questions. Time-series data has been wanting, and as a result, those who contribute to the long-run growth literature have been forced to use evidence from a very recent past.

The Data Constraint

Data availability is a key reason the literature took the shape it did. The availability and the character of poverty numbers and economic statistics have shaped the historical analysis of poverty and growth in sub-Saharan Africa. Broadening the tableau by adding more time-series data and revealing the implications of all this new empirical work is the key purpose of chapters 3, 4 and 5, which discuss economic growth, taxation, and living standards, respectively. Expanding the database will arguably change the formulation of the key research questions in African economic history. The quantitative histories of economic growth that use time-series data typically use 1960 or a more recent year as Year 1. The availability of this evidence partially explains why economists have focused on the postcolonial period. But for those who write histories of poverty using the dollar-per-day metric, 1990 is Year 1. Both are, of course, artificial starting points, but data availability restricts us to this time frame and to the kinds of questions that can be investigated.

Similarly, narratives of trends in living standards in Africa are shaped by the current configuration of what constitutes poverty knowledge, particularly at the World Bank, and what does not. That may be a mistake because the brief history of poverty by numbers in Africa is characterized by gaps and inaccuracies in the underlying data and because it fails to contextualize the history of poverty in the 1990s and 2000s in a longer time perspective. The result is that persistent chronic poverty became the "imagined fact" that prompted the narrative on Africa and poverty.

One of the central challenges is connecting the colonial period to the postcolonial period. When this is done, there is a conspicuous absence in the central narrative of the economic history of twentieth-century Africa. In previous analytical models, the postcolonial period has been treated as an "outcome" (and a dismal one) and a historical event in the colonial or the precolonial period has been treated as a root cause of this outcome. The aggregate pattern, particularly in terms of poverty and growth – although it is also evident in taxation measures – is a prolonged period of growth from the 1890s into the 1970s. This gave way to widespread failure and decline in the 1980s, followed by two decades of expansion since the late 1990s. Thus, it seems increasingly evident that growth failure in the postcolonial period has taken up undue space in explanations of African economic development. The old pattern in the literature was to regard the postcolonial period as a dismal outcome as evidenced by a low GDP per capita today that should be explained by a colonial or precolonial event or variable.

But instead of focusing on such trajectories of growth and seeking to explain them, economists took an analytical shortcut in the second generation of the growth literature. In their defense, the shortcut was necessitated by the paucity of evidence, but it did lead them astray. The new regressions stopped using growth measured as the percentage rate of change in GDP as evidence and switched to explaining country-level variations in income as measured by GDP per capita today. But when is "today"? For most of these regressions, "today" was the year 2000. As already noted, in principle the link the economic growth literature made between growth and income is relatively straightforward: Low income today must be the result of a lack of income growth in the past. The next step is more complicated. Because the evidence does not go very far back in time, the growth regression literature has not provided any evidence that actually explains any differences in long-term growth rates. We are meant to take a leap of faith that the distribution of GDP per capita in the year 2000 contains some cumulative difference that regressions can exploit to tease out some wisdom about why some countries have been successful and others have not.

Besides data availability, the type of data, the type of categories, and the mode of observation also matter. A central criticism of much of African history is that "the visions of Africa often derive from Europe and come still predominantly from the Western World. Our perception of the African past has always been a European perception" (Vansina, 1986: 40). Thus, when interpreting social and economic change in African societies, it is particularly important to assess the bias and subjectivity of the individuals who produced these sources. Administrators and explorers made observations using pre-1900 categories. The early scholarly observations are also dated. The racial and political views of those scholars shaped the type of information they gathered and how they categorized it. The basic question is whether the knowledge gained through these sources is useful at all. The discipline of African history has long recognized these problems, and economists who are seeking to contribute to the interpretation of the African past would do well to listen to the caveats of their historian counterparts.

The scholarly production of the persistence literature on African development has been built upon a compression of history to correlates between questionable data points in the past and evidence from a very recent past. Yet that literature prompted scholars to go to the sources and into the archives, and we are now able to piece together a picture of African economic development in the twentieth century that challenges some of the basic starting points in the persistence literature. New datasets might enable us to push the boundary of investigation back to allow for evaluations of trajectories of economic development across the colonial and postcolonial periods.

2 | *Seeing Like an African State in the Twentieth Century*

This book is not only data centric, it is also primarily based on descriptive statistics, and while it makes many substantive points about the trends in economic growth and shifts in living standards in sub-Saharan Africa during the twentieth century, I note several caveats. Although this chapter will dive further into the issue of "seeing like an African state" in the twentieth century, it is important to state that what is visible to states is limited. The omniscient state does not exist today and the colonial states had a very limited reach.

The focus on the postcolonial and the colonial states is not to be read as a dismissal of the importance of the precolonial period. Of course, there have been efforts to quantify economic change in the precolonial period, in particular focusing on the slave trade and currency circulation (such as, but not limited to, Curtin 1975, Ewald 1992, Hogendorn and Gemery 1988, Hogendorn and Johnson 1986, Johnson, 1970. Manning, 1983, Miers and Roberts, 1988.[1] Efforts to measure economic change preceding the colonial period are discussed in the chapter on economic growth, but for reasons of scope the main emphasis of this work is the shift of the "Year 1" back to the late nineteenth century, which I view as an improvement on time series that take Year 1 as 1960 or 1980. It is nonetheless still important that this should not be read as if economic change in the precolonial period or the efforts to study it do not matter. This is one of the factors limiting "seeing like an African state" in the twentieth century.

Yet, my view is that it is not necessary to know everything to know something. The chapters here are based on state records, which are of course frequently misleading. Reading state records as the "history" of the twentieth century would produce the kind of history from commanding heights that Bertolt Brecht's 1935 poem "Questions from a worker who reads," warns against. In that poem, a worker asks whether Caesar did not have a cook with him when he conquered the Gauls and whether the kings hauled the rocks for their monuments themselves. A similar warning comes from Harari (2014), who notes that archeologists might have been misleading us when they named the Stone Age, as it should probably have been called the wood age. However, wooden tools are not preserved in the archaeological record, while stone tools are.

The estimates of GDP growth presented here using colonial data views development through a very limited lens. We need to take very seriously the constraints of the data – what we see and what we do not see. Because this work is built on state records, we need to consider carefully what seeing like a state across the twentieth century looked like. The aim of collecting state records is to enable scholars to make comparisons across time and space, to provide perspectives that have not yet been considered in the absence of such descriptive data. While the data certainly has weaknesses, I propose that the insights the datasets provide are changing our vantage points on African economic history in fundamental ways.

A striking example of the power of datasets and the importance of vantage point comes from the debate on global warming. It took so long to notice global warming because of weaknesses in the global mean temperature dataset (Maslin, 2004: 27). In the 1970s, the data series went back only a few decades, and from that viewpoint it looked like temperatures had been falling since the 1940s. But the current dataset, which covers the period 1860–2010, shows that the temperatures are indeed on an upward trend.

When you do not have a complete picture, your impression may be biased. Every cross-country growth regression starts with the goal of using a global sample, but because of incomplete data availability, some countries are excluded from the equations. The assumption that a country's lack of ability or opportunity to conduct a household survey is not correlated with any other determinants of poverty and slow growth is a brave one. Continent-wide statements on recent economic growth and trends in poverty are based on observations from a small subset of the world's nations. Sometimes international organizations make up the missing observations to fill in the gaps when datasets are assembled; other times economists extrapolate data from neighboring countries to fill in data for a country that has no data to contribute (Jerven, 2013: 8–32).[2]

The word *statistics* derives from French and German words that mean "of the state." The work presented here and indeed perhaps the majority of the work published by economic historians of Africa rests on the official records of the colonial and the postcolonial state – that is, information about the state and information created by the states. This lens gives a particular view. The reach of states is limited and thus the statistics they create are lacking in availability and quality. In response to this dearth of solid information, particularly for precolonial Africa, those who study African history and economic history have always used a multitude of sources (Parker and Rathbone, 2007). Arguably this methodological innovation has been one of the most defining contributions the study of Africa has made to the discipline of history as a whole; it is perhaps best presented in Jan Vansina's (1982) article "Towards a history of lost corners in the world."

My reading of the historiography on African economic development as presented in Chapter 1 emphasized how the nature and availability of evidence has shaped the literature. The clearest takeaway from the new evidence presented on economic growth, taxation, and livings standard in chapters 3, 4 and 5 is that it radically changes the main interpretation of economic development in Africa in the twentieth century.

Of course, a slightly different connotation of the word *statistics* could be "by the state." Such an interpretation reminds the reader and the researcher that state records are not universal or random samples. Looking through state records does not provide a clear, objective view of the past. This is of course true in all studies, but it applies particularly to the study of colonial empires, a context where the information has been carefully curated and is very selective.

Why Do States Count?

In his continued efforts to understand the actions of the modern state, James Scott (1998) implores us to see like one. The state, as Scott famously argues, strives to "make a society legible" (1998: 2). He deems legibility to be the "central problem in statecraft" (2). In this vein, Scott argues that the state's efforts to document, map, and measure the natural and social worlds are part of a larger endeavor to transform it. Such records and statistics and their associated practices are necessarily "state simplifications" (3) that are rendered legible to the reader through the metaphor of the map and cartography. These simplifications can be fully understood only when one assumes the narrowed viewpoint of the state (11). The practices this viewpoint is embedded in attempt to bring measurability, uniformity, and predictability to natural and social phenomena that were formerly out of the state's reach. As deliberate simplifications, however, they are "thin" (44): they miss much of what they purport to capture.

Scott argues that the drive to map the natural and social world is not confined to regimes at a particular point on the political spectrum, to a particular state's geography or history, to its status as a colony, or to any other variable. It is intrinsically tied to the history of state making and, crucially for Scott, to increasingly ambitious state intervention during the modern era. He narrates the growth of state-led measurement and standardization, from "scientific forestry" in eighteenth-century Prussia to the contemporaneous "metrical revolution" in France (11, 30). The forceful imposition of the metric system, Scott argues, went beyond rational measurement toward a broader transformative goal of forging a "rational citizenry" – the creation of "a single people" (32).

These attempts at social engineering on unprecedented scales rested on a particular view on the part of state that forged deliberate simplifications that ordered and reordered the world toward intervention. It was bolstered by an increasing confidence in the "objectivity" of science and its link to modernist aims of an ever-extending road to progress. This resonates strongly with Alain Desrosières's contemporaneous work *The Politics of Large Numbers* (1998), which looks at the history of statistics and how "social facts become things" (2). Desrosières also links the history of statistics to state building, noting that "statistics is connected with the construction of the state, with its unification and administration" (8). He argues that the increasing power of the statistical "fact," even when it is enmeshed in particular historical practices, is bolstered by two forms of authority: Science and the state (17). Rather ambiguously, for Desrosières, as for Scott, state power is both a condition and a product of "know[ing] a nation" (16).

Although Desrosières examines the development of statistical reasoning from the early modern era in diverse settings such as Great Britain, Germany, and the United States, he gives particular attention to France as a pathbreaker in statistical descriptions. In pre-Revolution France, the power of the monarch was strong in a relatively centralized regime. This meant that early analysis in France was "conducted from the point of view of the king and his power" (27). Desrosières identifies the French Revolution as the critical moment in statistical development in a truly modern sense. In the postrevolutionary moment, conditions were conducive to the rapid, indeed "spectacular" (31) formation of political and administrative tools in a wide range of areas in a very short time: This is Scott's "metric revolution" (31). At the heart of this drive was the consolidation of the state, not least existentially: "The most visible manifestation of this process of homogenizing and codifying many aspects of human existence was the unification of the national territory" (32).

Theodore Porter (1996) also pays close attention to the generation of objectified knowledge that is enmeshed in contingent practices in particular scientific communities. For Porter, "day-to-day science is at least as much about the transmission of skills and practices as about the establishment of theoretical doctrines" (12). He maps the role of multiple, intersecting dynamics and actors in creating "objective" numbers in the modern era. His analysis affords more power and independence to research institutes and professional groups, for example. He underscores the role capitalism and market forces played in unifying and simplifying measures through the development of large-scale trading networks (25). Later intergovernmental organizations played a key role in such dynamics (31). Such networks are truly globalized, working above, below, and yes, through the state toward something of a more "collective product" (12) of objectified numbers.

Porter attends to the enduring and powerful influence of the increasingly bureaucratic state in the birth and evolution of statistics. He notes a drive "to transform the world that science purports to describe" (17). Measurement that simplifies and describes was central to the nascent hard sciences and in turn to contemporaneous state-building (17–19). For Porter, such measurement "aspired to independence from local customs and local knowledge" (22) that formed a part of the centralizing state, and he highlights the role of the French Revolution as a "signal event" for the unification of measures on the continent (25). As both Desrosières and Scott do, Porter sees state power as both a product and a condition of the standardization of measurement and classification. On the one hand, such standardization enhanced administrative control, but on the other, "an impressive display of state power" was required to enact and enforce it (26). For Porter, such wielding of power must be married to a legitimate ideology, be it that of revolution or of empire.

The literature on seeing like an African state is not as developed as the literature on the use of statistics and how it developed side by side with the growth of the modern state. My previous work sparked an academic debate that also resulted in a special editorial titled "The economics of contemporary Africa" in *Annales* in 2016. As the piece noted, "For the social sciences, numbers and figures are at once fascinating and ambiguous. Their validity is often fragile, always open to challenges, but their claim to precision (real or apparent) means that they carry a considerable power of suggestion." However, how numbers are produced and to what degree they are capable of describing the social and economic reality remains an open question (Annales, 2016: 503). In that issue, three scholars discuss the questions my book *Poor Numbers* (Jerven, 2013) raised.

Economist Agnès Labrousse (2016) is mainly concerned about the validity of numbers, the perspective of the numbers, and who they are relevant for. Labrousse takes issue with some of the economic perspectives and argues that many economists today have gone beyond the simple measures of GDP and the like as direct links to development and growth. Nevertheless, she admits that these figures are still dominant in the development discourse, not only by themselves but also because they form a key component in determining the United Nations Development Programme's Human Development Index (HDI) and other rankings. She takes issue with generalizations about a continent based on data that she claims has a skewed bias toward former British colonies and does not pay enough attention to the differences among various regions. For example, she points to former French colonies and the work done by French scholars to combine the qualitative and the quantitative in what she labels "The French tradition" (523).

In his article "Studying Africa's large numbers," Boris Samuel (2016) echoes some of these concerns about the reliability and validity of figures, but he is concerned about the sociological foundations behind the figures and how various actors create, understand, and use numbers. According to Samuel, an analysis that values the statistical chain, arguing that numbers are a construct from a range of actors – and to some extent also figures that are open for negotiations (577, 570). Samuel's core argument is that social and historical context is essential;

he argues for a more fine-grained understanding and says that in the case of international comparison they should be "recontextualized within the history of economic governance in Africa" (576).

Dennis Cogneau (2016a) questions if it is even possible to measure and draw standard economic conclusions because of the poor quality of data in Africa. In this, he echoes some of my core arguments in *Poor Numbers*. However, he emphasizes that although there might be some questions about methodology in newer microeconomic studies, including household studies, they could provide a broader spectrum of information if they are used cautiously. Cogneau cautions against the classic economic approach, mainly because of the low quality of data, but he also argues that in any case such an approach would provide only a piece of the puzzle, as very little attention has been paid to the development of economic history (and the history of growth) in Africa. He argues that we need more comparative studies to complement existing knowledge, especially comparative work in Africa, as such studies have "the advantage of highlighting intriguing scientific mysteries that call out to be resolved, even as they challenge grand narratives based on hasty generalizations" (556).

Blue Books, Colonial Records, and the Postcolonial Record

Naturally, administrators and rulers have a need to know the state and condition of their territory. The blue books of the British Empire took this to a whole new level. They are the key source of this book; they shed new light on a part of history that is seemingly somewhat forgotten.

Today, the national accounts for the United Kingdom are still recorded in blue books. This convention extends back to the British colonies in the nineteenth and twentieth centuries. Economic historians have used blue books extensively (Frankema and van Waijenburg, 2012). From the 1820s to the end of the 1950s, these books recorded information that was invaluable for running a vast empire. They contain detailed information on taxation, population, geographical changes, prospects and challenges for the colonial government, and so on. These records are also a great source for information about a variety of other issues such as health, literacy, trade, and much more. Naturally, one must keep in mind that these records were written and the information in them was collected with the double intention of satisfying the metropole's need for information and creating a tool for the local colonial government. Although that context is important for analyzing these sources, they still contain a remarkable resource for scholars interested in economic history and the social sciences. The magnitude of the volumes grew over time, as a result of the growth of the colonial government and the British government's demand for more information. Even though the amount of detail in some of these books is astonishing, we should always pay attention to what information was excluded even as the blue books grew in size. Despite their obvious bias, they have remained a partly untapped source of information in the discourse on the history of African development until fairly recently.

Entering an archive and leafing through blue books gives one a perspective about what got recorded and what did not. The blue books for the Gambia offer some representative examples. The earliest blue books for this country date from 1828. These early volumes are very slim. Until the 1890s, blue books for the Gambia cover only trading posts or port cities. As the decades passed, the UK's control of territory increased. There were more items to enter and the volumes increased in size. The table of contents grew and the categories became more aggregated. In the nineteenth century, some volumes recorded the exact amount of haberdashery that was imported and at what price. This level of detail later disappeared in favor of more general items.

The record for the Gambia consists of the items that were of interest to colonial administrators. The emphasis was on state revenue and expenditures, numbers and types of staff, pensions, wages, and the external trade record. Internal trade or food production is absent, and data on other types of production are also largely missing from the blue books. These categories of information appeared in other colonial state records, although in French West Africa, there was more focus on recording data about food production and food security, perhaps because the French colonies were situated more in arid and semi-arid areas than British and Portuguese colonies were (Bonnecase, 2009).

National accounting is associated with the dawn of independence, when the GDP estimates were reported to international agencies using their standardized formulas (Ward, 2004). On paper, the reporting was universal in coverage, but in practice many data gaps remained

(Jerven, 2013). Colonial GDP estimates do exist for both French and British areas (Bonnecase, 2015), but at the end of colonial rule there was more effort to include estimates of African production, whereas estimates in settler colonies such as Rhodesia only focused on the colonial economy. Thus, there was a move toward new types of survey and data collection items, as the administrative records alone did not suffice to record the economies. Ghana is perhaps one of the examples that most clearly illustrates these points from this period. As the first country to gain independence in 1957, it was also in the forefront of census taking as a tool for the new and independent government. Ghana is an interesting case with regard to the tools and methods of surveys and counting both before and after independence. Gerardo Serra (2014) demonstrates through an investigation of a series of household budget surveys in the 1950s that the typical household is particularly difficult to frame in a correct way that corresponds to the realities throughout a country. He writes of how selectiveness due to limitations of capacity and political interest resulted in what he terms "an uneven statistical topography" (Serra 2014). This unevenness has both spatial and conceptual dimensions. The spatial dimension refers to sampling choices that were based on economic considerations, statistical capacity, and access. The colonial government of Ghana did not have the resources for or interest in counting the entire colony in a statistically satisfying way. This mirrored the government's uneven control over different parts of the country. Household surveys generally favored more densely populated areas in the south. However, one survey that related to cocoa production took a different approach as the key in that case was to understand the economic dynamic: This survey differed both in the conceptual and the geographical approach. The conceptual dimension relates to the various tools and measurements surveyors used depending on the political agenda and the economic interests in the areas being surveyed. For instance, Serra finds that surveys of household budgets tended to focus on expenditures and paid far less attention to the composition of household income (10). Despite the shortcomings Serra describes, Ghanaian surveys still provide valuable insights, and some of them penetrated rural areas about which the colonial government had little information. However, the design of these surveys and the adaptations colonial surveyors made to them necessitate a careful consideration of the historical and political context in which they were conducted. They were part of a political play that reflected the interests of the colonizers.

In the newly independent African states, there was a demand for more information about countries, populations, and future prospects. This was seen as a necessity for modernization and state building. At the same time, governments and statisticians wanted to distance statistical work in the new nations from how census taking was done during the colonial area (Serra, 2018). Ghana, which achieved independence in 1957, spearheaded this effort with its remarkable census of 1960. Serra (2018) focuses on "conceptualizing the relationship between the census and the building of the nation-state as mediated by the creation of public trust" (663). Ghana was the first independent state in Africa (south of Sahara) to undertake a census that was designed to be part of the United Nations' World Population and Housing Census Programme of 1960. Unlike previous censuses, a "modern census" required a shift in the population's understanding of what a census actually meant. It was imperative for the new government to highlight the positive aspects of the census and distance it from the perception among some that it was a tool for laying the foundation for taxation. Serra demonstrates how Ghana's new government mounted a "census education and enlightenment campaign" in the months before the census to generate support for the census and to connect it to national identity and support for President Kwame Nkrumah. Serra draws on media coverage to show that this campaign effectively redefined the census as a vehicle for national identity, in contrast to the United Nations' push to cast national censuses as a strictly technocratic and scientific exercise.

How Good Are States at Counting? The Census Record

The census record of course has a direct relationship to any per capita statements a government can make, but it can also be a good indication of what states were able to control and register over time and space (Lee and Zhang, 2013). Statistics play a role in all levels of decision making because numbers are perceived to be "scientific" and objective. Census taking is one way of measuring state capacity and state presence or at the very least of gauging how seriously we should take other state records. While having a census is obviously important, a state's ability to take a census is limited by its interest and strength.

Demographic data enables governments to estimate human capital and consequently to allocate resources among regions and communities in order to provide adequate funding for education, sanitary infrastructure, and health care, among other issues. Detailed numbers are needed to assess and evaluate projects and policies over time in order to understand whether such resource allocations are effective. More generally, regular census data permits states to track change over time and make meaningful projections of patterns and trends. Measuring change over time is an indispensable feature of any project or study, be it by economic scholars, development agencies, administrators, engineers, or anthropologists, and a census with a broad scope can become a base year in statistical calculations or sampling frame for future surveys.

Politicians' need for nationwide statistics might have helped drive the surge in African censuses in the early 1960s. The advent of elections mattered: Boundaries of electoral districts are usually determined by the distribution of the population, which can only be accurately measured through a census.

The main objective of this section is to trace the number of statistically reliable censuses that have been undertaken on the African continent. Etienne Van de Walle attempted to create such a database in 1968. Dominique Tabutin and Bruno Schoumaker made a second attempt in 2004. A decade later, Ewout Frankema and I attempted to evaluate the accuracy of colonial population estimates (Frankema and Jerven 2014). A number of early bibliographies on African statistical publications exist (Population Research Center, 1965, 1968; Pinfold, 1985), but they do not contain any information beyond the title, location, and year of the publications. However, Domschke and Goyer (1986) provide accounts of each individual census, which has proved invaluable for determining their credibility. Robert Kuczynski's demographic survey of the British colonial empire is also an excellent resource (Kuczynski, 1948).

A major political change can lead to different accounts of the reliability of a census. Employees of a new regime will accuse the previous regime of producing faulty numbers or omitting regions. For example, Statistics South Africa points toward 1996 as the year of the first "democratic census" and accuses previous enumerations of not including the large African population living in homelands (Simelane, 2002). Other sources confirm that South African censuses did cover the entirety of the nation's territory and population (Domschke and Goyer, 1986). It matters greatly whether reliable data on the South African population existed before 1996 when a government or a scholar is assessing historic changes and comparing them with demographic trends today. Whether South Africa has had eleven universal censuses, as Domschke and Goyer claim, or only three reliable ones, as statistics officials argue, of course affects our assessment of the South African state's capacity to count. In cases like this, in-depth analysis has to be made to compare what a range of primary and secondary sources say about a particular census in order to assess whether it should be considered a reliable source of data.

As of July 2019, at least 275 adequately reliable censuses had taken place on the African continent.[3] In addition, a comparable number of smaller demographic surveys and unreliable or unpublished censuses exist.

Table 2.1 *Number of censuses per country*

Algeria	9	Gabon	4	Rwanda	4
Angola	5	Gambia	8	São Tomé and Príncipe	8
Benin	4	Ghana	5	Senegal	4
Botswana	7	Guinea	3	Seychelles	8
Burkina Faso	4	Guinea-Bissau	5	Sierra Leone	5
Burundi	3	Kenya	6	Somalia	0
Cameroon	3	Lesotho	9	South Africa	11
Cape Verde	8	Liberia	3	Sudan	4
Central African Republic	3	Libya	5	South Sudan	3
Chad	2	Madagascar	3	Swaziland (Eswatini)	6
Comoros	4	Malawi	6	Tanzania	6
Congo (Republic of)	3	Mali	4	Togo	3
Congo (DRC)	1	Mauritania	4	Tunisia	8
Cote d'Ivoire	3	Mauritius	12	Uganda	7
Djibouti	1	Morocco	6	Western Sahara	2
Egypt	11	Mozambique	7	Zambia	5
Equatorial Guinea	9	Namibia	6	Zimbabwe	4
Eritrea	1	Niger	3		
Ethiopia	3	Nigeria	4	Total (n = 55)	275

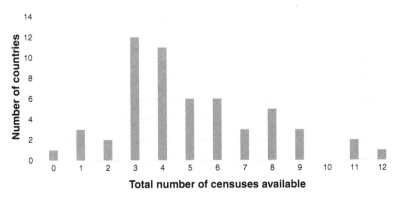

Figure 2.1 Distribution of census frequency per country

A large majority of countries have held between three and six censuses, which, depending on the temporal distribution, is sufficient to allow some measurement of change over time. However, the period in which the censuses were taken affects their value in terms of understanding projections of developments and changes. The United Nations has determined that there should be a maximum of ten years between censuses to enable complete interpretation of the data. Of the thirty-seven countries that had four or more censuses, twenty-nine followed the criteria of regular periodicity by having at least one census for each of the past three census rounds, a term the UN Population Fund defines as a decennial period spanning from years ending with the number five to years ending with the number four.[4] This is an improvement in data availability, but there is still a long way to go, especially among some of the poorest and most conflict-ridden countries.

A few countries have a long history of regular census taking. This allows for robust historical analysis and highly accurate accounts of their demographic development. These states, which I am calling the outlier states, cluster into three regional groups: North Africa, the small island states in the Indian and Atlantic oceans, and South Africa plus the sparsely inhabited countries in southern Africa.

As Table 2.2 indicates, these three clusters of outlier countries have on average around twice the demographic statistical depth as that of the remainder of the countries on the continent. It is not difficult to make qualified guesses about why this is the case; a smaller geographic and demographic size seems to matter, as is seen with the island states and the small populations in southern Africa. Greater economic and

Table 2.2 *African states with a high density of censuses*

	North Africa n = 5	Island States n = 6	Southern Africa+[1] n = 5	Remainder of Africa n = 39
Average number of censuses	7.8	7.2	7.8	3.9

[1] South Africa, Eswatini, Botswana, Lesotho, Namibia.

geopolitical importance and greater wealth matters too, both before and after independence, as is the case with the countries in North Africa and southern Africa.

In general, a country's economic and geopolitical importance is worth taking into consideration when assessing the number of censuses. Not surprisingly, the countries with the fewest censuses tend to be some of the poorest and most fragile states, such as Somalia, the Democratic Republic of the Congo, Chad, Madagascar, and Eritrea. In addition, unrest and civil wars are an obvious hindrance to carrying out the field work needed for a census. One of the most notable examples of a statistically disrupted country is Angola, which had four solid decennial censuses from 1940 to 1970 under Portuguese rule but did not have a single complete enumeration after that because of civil war and unrest until May 2014, when it completed its first census in decades.

Distribution of African Censuses over Time

Figure 2.2 presents the year of the first census in a country and visualizes a number of noteworthy features. The graph plots the number of countries that have already had their first census per year. There were many incomplete demographic counts, such as the decennial censuses in most French colonies that included only European settlers. Such surveys are not of much value in explaining a country's demographic development until the present time. The few countries that did conduct universal censuses early on all fall in the three groups of outliers already presented: island states, colonies in southern Africa, and colonies in North Africa. The early debut of these censuses partly explains why these countries have such a comparatively high total number.

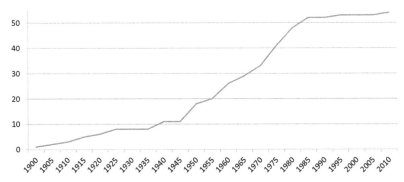

Figure 2.2 Number of countries that have had their first census

In 1940, the Portuguese colonial administration decided to commence decennial enumeration in most of its African colonies. This ended up being the beginning of the most complete statistical recordings of any of the colonial powers. By 1940, the other colonial powers were greatly occupied with matters more pressing than enumerating their colonies. For example, Domschke and Goyer (1986) note that the censuses in a number of British colonies were postponed until the end of World War II. This trend is directly reflected in Figure 2.2, as no new countries undertook censuses in the period 1940–1945.

After World War II, Britain began to conduct censuses in an increasing number of its African colonies. By 1960 (a frequently used reference point for independence), twenty-six of the fifty-five countries had counted their population at least once. Unfortunately for national administrators, scholars, and populations, a substantial number of countries still had not conducted a census well into the 1970s. This means that in those countries, accurate information about changes in population size, religious composition, literacy rates, urbanization levels, and occupations are not known.

Table 2.3 shows that colonies that had high European settler rates tend to have more census-based data. Comparing the census data from larger numbers of African countries reveals other commonalities, such as which nation colonized the country. Countries that had previously been colonized by Belgium or France were latecomers to census taking, for example. Seventeen of the twenty countries that did not take a census before 1974 were former Belgian and French colonies (the other three were Ethiopia, Eritrea, and Somalia). This reveals a seemingly strong correlation between early postcolonial statistical

Table 2.3 *Average number of censuses by colonial rule and time period*

Colonial Rule	France	UK	Portugal	Belgium	Spain	Other
Number of colonies	21	18	5	3	2	6
Censuses per country before independence	0.7	1.2	3.4	0	3.5	1.5
Censuses per country after independence	3.2	4.5	2.8	2.7	1.5	4
Censuses per country by 1960	0.7	1.3	2.6	0	2.5	0.3
Total number of censuses per country	3.9	5.7	6.2	2.7	5	2.8

capacity and the colonizer, indicating a difference in statistical infrastructure set up during colonial rule. Statistical capacity is likely one of the consequences of the type of institutional infrastructure former colonizers create. This institution-based reasoning falls in line with the argument of Acemoğlu et al. (2001) and could account for the clear differences in censuses between nations that were colonized by Belgium at one extreme and settler colonies in southern and northern Africa at the other.

Some explanations for differences in the postcolonial record of census taking can be seen as a legacy of colonial rule. British colonies had a higher degree of indirect rule and a common-law system that emphasized private property and the contract between the individual and the state. These factors increased the attention British authorities paid to colonial subjects. In contrast, French (and to some extent Belgian and Portuguese) colonies encouraged the creation of a "civilized" (European-assimilated) elite and highly centralized institutions founded on civil law (La Porta et al., 1999; Bolt and Bezemer, 2009). Based on these premises, some of the differences in colonial legacies presented in Table 2.3 are likely accounted for by the higher degree of attention French authorities paid to the European elite than to the remaining colonial subjects in French colonies. One can infer from these factors that France had little incentive to take censuses during the colonial era. As a result, newly independent countries that were former French colonies lacked experience in conducting censuses and were ill equipped to undertake the task.

Statistically, these assumptions appear to be accurate. Table 2.3 shows countries organized by the colonial power they were ruled by for the majority of their colonial period. It is evident that a marked difference existed between the efforts colonial powers exerted to enumerate their colonies. Because African countries gained independence in different years, I have used the number of censuses that existed by 1960 as a common reference point. As mentioned, Portugal commenced regular universal enumerations in its colonies in 1940 and 1950. This provided the Portuguese colonial administration with knowledge of its colonial populace that was unparalleled in its accuracy and was based on a statistical foundation.

Although the British Empire regularly released accounts that included its colonial populations, these figures were generally based on estimates. However, even though this data was not subjected to vigorous and detailed recording during the colonial period, countries that were former British colonies fared the best after independence. They conducted an average of 4.5 censuses per country over the five decades after the British possessions in Africa were dismantled. The trend in Figure 2.2 is confirmed in Table 2.3: Both France and Belgium appear to have been indifferent to the accuracy of their colonial numbers. No former French or Belgian colonies except for Tunisia, Algeria, Comoros, and Mauritius, ever experienced a universal census under colonial rule. This means that until recently, most of the continent between the Sahara and the Kalahari were gray zones of statistically uncharted territory.

As mentioned, a majority of all African countries (twenty-nine of fifty-four) now have an unbroken record for the last three census rounds. The rest, however, have experienced scattered and irregular censuses.

What Do African States Count?

One of the striking problems in assessing the recent growth in sub-Saharan Africa is not only the actual rate of economic growth but also how this growth is distributed and whether it is inclusive. So what happens to poverty during growth? The most important metric of poverty, judging purely in terms of influence, is the headcount of the number of people living in poverty. The data needed to create this measure has been collected through Living Standard Measurement

Surveys under the auspices of the World Bank.[5] The first Living Standard Measurement Survey was held in Côte D'Ivoire in 1985. Thus, the history of poverty by numbers is very short.

For historians of Africa, the history is really a bit longer. John Iliffe's *The African Poor: A History* (1987) is an instructive example. It is fundamentally interested in unearthing historical causes of poverty. To address that question, Iliffe traces and defines the different forms poverty has taken over time and space in Africa using tools of the linguistic and document historian. In his interpretation, because poverty is multidimensional, it defies simple quantification (not to mention advanced econometric testing). Quantification would be of limited value because the appropriate data are not available.[6] Even if they were, they would potentially capture both structural poverty, or poverty caused by personal or social circumstances, and conjunctural poverty, or temporary poverty brought about by a crisis (Iliffe 1987: 4). By examining the history of poverty, Iliffe identified plausible patterns of causality without using historical observations on poverty to determine causality statistically or with the use of numbers.

Figure 2.3 shows that only about a quarter of the countries in sub-Saharan Africa have conducted four or more poverty surveys since the 1980s. According to the most recent World Bank report on the topic, as of 2012 only twenty-five of forty-eight countries had conducted at least two surveys over the past decade. Five countries that represent about 5 percent of the African population have no data at all for measuring poverty (Beegle et al., 2016). Scholars may still be bold and say something about long continent-wide trends. For instance, I have documented how Sala-i-Martín and Pinkovskiy (2010) claim that African poverty is decreasing much faster than we think (Jerven, 2015). They claim that African poverty decreased steadily from 1995 until 2006. They did not have annual poverty data for all countries for this period, so they matched GDP growth data from the Penn World Table with inequality data from the UNU-WIDER World Income Inequality Database.[7] They report that they considered 118 surveys for forty-eight countries. This may seem like a lot of surveys, but on average, it is only just above two data points per country for a study that makes claims regarding the direction and rate of change in monetary poverty for the period 1970 to 2006. In fact, for this period of thirty-six years, thirty-six annual observations should have been completed for each of

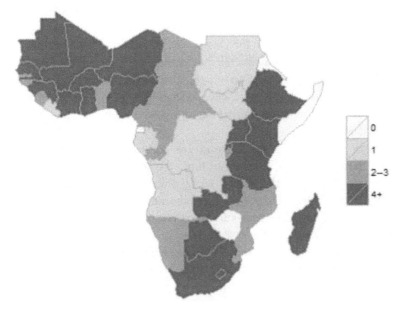

Figure 2.3 Number of poverty surveys conducted in sub-Saharan Africa, 2003–2012
Map generated by data from the World Bank Group, PovcalNet, http://ire search.worldbank.org/PovcalNet/povOnDemand.aspx

the forty-eight countries, which means that 1,610 observations are missing from their dataset. According to their database, no observations exist on poverty after 2004, so the recent trend they identify is based entirely on conjecture.

Data on poverty are missing entirely for large countries such as Angola and the Democratic Republic of the Congo, and thus the continent-wide trends are based on biased material. There are no data points for Angola, Congo, Comoros, Cape Verde, the Democratic Republic of the Congo, Eritrea, Equatorial Guinea, Seychelles, Togo, São Tomé and Príncipe, Chad, Liberia, and Sudan. In addition, six countries have only one survey, and you need at least two data points to draw a line. There are no data from the most recent decade, and the omissions of the big countries are glaring. It would still perhaps be acceptable to produce a poverty study on the handful of countries for which we have on average more than one observation per decade, such as Côte d'Ivoire, Ethiopia, Ghana, Gambia, Kenya, Madagascar, Mauritania, Nigeria, and Zambia, but to pretend that there is a poverty line in countries where we have no data is deceptive. Sala-i-Martín and Pinkovskiy (2010) even produced a graph of poverty lines in the Democratic Republic of the Congo from 1970 to 2006, but they do not tell their readers that there is absolutely no evidence at all underlying the graph. One is left wondering whether a researcher would get away with presenting a thirty-year poverty or inequality trend in Sweden using data borrowed from Germany, Spain, or Ireland.

More generally, figures 2.4 and 2.5 highlight that the dearth of information available to us is not limited to the collection of poverty statistics. First, in the thirty years since USAID introduced its Demographic Health Survey in sub-Saharan Africa, forty-three countries in the region have been surveyed. Within these forty-three countries, twelve (one-quarter of countries in sub-Saharan Africa) were surveyed more than five times. On the other hand, ten of the forty-eight countries conducted fewer than two surveys, restricting our

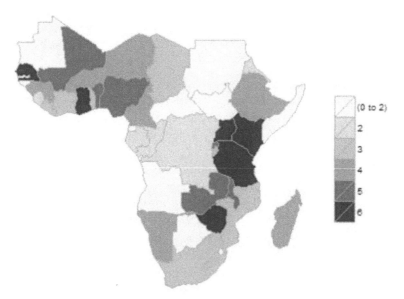

Figure 2.4 Number of demographic and health surveys conducted in sub-Saharan Africa since 1986
Map generated by data from USAID, Demographic and Health Surveys, https://dhsprogram.com

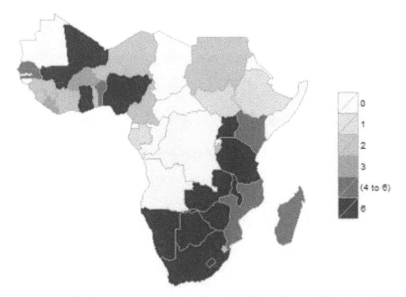

Figure 2.5 Afrobarometer surveys conducted in sub-Saharan Africa since 1999
Map generated by data from Afrobarometer, https://afrobarometer.org

ability to make any comparisons across time. Included in this group are five countries (Guinea Bissau, Mauritius, Seychelles, Somalia, and South Sudan, which represent roughly 2.7 percent of the total population of sub-Saharan Africa) that have yet to participate in the survey program.

Afrobarometer has conducted surveys on a variety of issues in six waves since 1999.[8] While all twelve of the original countries surveyed have participated in the subsequent five waves, the rest of the continent has been slower to participate. While thirty-three of the forty-eight countries in sub-Saharan Africa participated in the most recent wave, only twenty countries participated in wave number four. Overall, eighteen countries in sub-Saharan Africa have participated in fewer than two waves of Afrobarometer surveys. Fifteen of those countries (which represent 16.7 percent of the population of sub-Saharan Africa) have not participated at all.[9]

Household surveys and other survey data that form the basis of the poverty numbers miss millions of poor individuals because of how they are designed. In turn, since the surveys are missing the poor, the sick, the nomadic, and people who are fleeing, only censuses can really

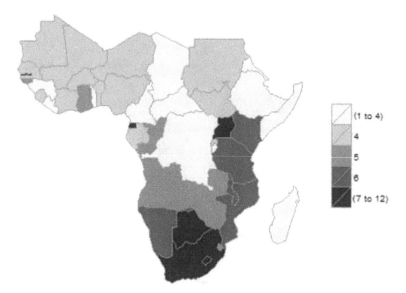

Figure 2.6 Number of censuses conducted per country in sub-Saharan Africa since 1900
Map generated by data from the United Nations Statistics Division (2015); Bonde (2012).

rectify biases in the data (Carr-Hill, 2016). However, as Figure 2.6 makes clear, census taking in sub-Saharan Africa has been sporadic and uneven. While it is difficult to make contemporary judgments, it is even more difficult if one goes back in time to write the history of demographic change in sub-Saharan Africa.

In his introduction to the second of two volumes of essays collected from two conferences on African historical demography in 1977 and 1981, economic historian Eric Wrigley neatly summed up the accomplishments to that date, the limitations of those findings, and the difficulties for the way ahead: "One thing, perhaps only one thing, is certain about African historical demography. It takes a bold and determined scholar to embark on the study of numbers, and of changes in numbers, in countries where until very recently nobody was even counting, let alone recording the results" (Wrigley, 1982).

For the precolonial period, the empirical evidence is so thin that it is illuminating to point to John Thornton's work on baptismal records from missionaries in the Kingdom of Kongo (Thornton, 1977). He found that the population in Kongo for the period 1650 to 1700 was much *lower* than commonly assumed (about 500,000 rather than two million). This suggests that the civil wars and slave trades of the seventeenth and eighteenth centuries had a much less disastrous impact on populations than has commonly been assumed. So while there are some precolonial data, there is too little to establish a firm and undisputed time series. Meanwhile, the colonial censuses are widely discredited and are not therefore authoritative benchmarks (Fetter, 1987). And although the populations of states in postcolonial Africa are better recorded, census taking has remained uneven, irregular, and incomplete (Tabutin and Schoumaker, 2004).

The problems of getting the total population right in the colonial period sometimes carried into the postcolonial periods. It has always been difficult to agree upon the total population figure for Nigeria. All of the censuses in Nigeria, from colonial times until the last one in 2006, have been heavily contested. Counting people in Nigeria is a striking example of the political economy of statistics. Nigeria gained independence between the population census the colonial authorities administered in 1953 and the nation's population census in 1962. In 1953, Nigerians correctly anticipated that the census would form the basis for estimating tax receipts. Thus, people wished not to be counted in 1952. In 1962, the situation was the opposite. The census would determine federal expenditures and political rights. The 1962 total population count was widely considered fraudulent and was rejected A new census was called for in 1963 and conducted the same year. The end result was a count of 30 million in 1953 and an almost doubling of that number to 56 million in 1963, implying an implausibly high growth rate. Since then, it has been impossible to agree upon the size and distribution of the population in Nigeria. In a recent report, *The Economist* claimed that Nigeria's population is massively exaggerated, by as much as 20 million (The Economist, 2015).

These are key weaknesses in the data, and they shape how development in Africa is explained. My argument is that to date, the data quality has not had a significant impact on how African economic history is interpreted. Particularly in recent times, scholars have made sweeping conclusions based on correlations between historical datasets and contemporary GDP estimates, although the latter in particular have been shown to be very soft indeed (Jerven, 2010c). However, the data constraint has been acutely felt in the lack of time-series data on the key variables. Without historical data on living standards, scholars have been compelled to take a leap of faith and think that if Africa is poor today, it was probably poor yesterday and the day before that. Hence, the purpose of the proposed models has been to explain this persistence and the question has been "Why is Africa so poor?" (Acemoğlu and Robinson, 2010). Because there is no reliable time-series data that can tell us whether countries in Africa tax more today than they did twenty years ago, much less fifty or one hundred years ago, the question has become, "Why do developing countries tax so little?" (Besley and Persson, 2014). Although the GDP growth series do not begin until the 1960s, some scholars proclaim that Africa is the tragedy of the entire twentieth century (Artadi and Sala-i-Martín, 2003) and some ask why there has been a chronic failure of growth in Africa (Collier and Gunning, 1999a, 1999b).

So it is perhaps time to see if we can find better data to try to come up with different, finer, and more granular questions that take account of the longitudinal and spatial variation in African wealth and poverty across the twentieth century in a more meaningful way. I will start by correcting the narrative of economic growth.

3 | New Data and New Perspectives on Economic Growth in Africa

Much of the evidence presented in this book rewrites the history of the economic development of African countries in the twentieth century. The centerpiece evidence in that history is economic growth, or movement in GDP per capita. When the evidence of economic growth in African economies is put in a global perspective, it becomes clear that that evidence is lacking in both reliability and availability. The research that underpins this chapter seeks to improve both of those aspects. The main contribution is to a new time series of GDP for a selection of colonies in Africa. Although there has been a recent surge in quantitative research on long-term economic development in Africa, the literature that purports to evaluate long-term economic performance often uses evidence from a very recent past.

Most of this literature has focused on establishing relationships between historical events and income levels today. This focus is a result of one basic data constraint: Estimates of national income and economic growth for African economies are only available as far back as 1960 or (in the Maddison dataset) from 1950. As a result, the economic growth literature that evaluates long-term economic performance often uses evidence from the very recent past. Typically, that literature focuses on explaining variation in income per capita today and asserts causal relationships across periods without being able to account for different trajectories of economic development. This has resulted in what has been called a compression of history (Austin, 2008). Focusing on explaining trajectories of African economic growth instead of explaining the lack of economic growth would be an improvement.

One argument is that because of different institutional configurations, African economies have been stuck in low growth. This is a testable proposition. To test it, it is necessary to have consistent and reliable estimates of economic change. Recently there have been efforts to provide historical national accounts data for a range of European and Asian economies (Jerven, 2010b). This chapter contributes to that literature by applying similar methods to Africa, offering new GDP series for a set of countries for the colonial period. In this chapter, I review the current databases and their shortcomings. I then review the existing historical national accounts estimates and present the state of the art in national accounts in African countries. Finally, I discuss some new estimates of historical national accounts and reassess our knowledge of the history of growth in African economies.

Current Databases of African Growth

Data availability is the chief constraint for those who study the history of economic growth in African economies. Because the history of economic growth has been constructed using data from databases, 1960 (in the World Development Indicators) or 1950 (in the Maddison dataset and part of the Penn World Table) is Year 1 in studies of economic growth in Africa. Thus, the history of economic growth in Africa has typically been written from the year of the starting date of the database. As a result, the first generation of studies of economic growth either focused on the period after 1960 or on the GDP per capita today as an outcome and did not use time-series data at all.

The availability of data has shaped the literature on African economic growth. For example, when Artadi and Sala-i-Martín (2003) wrote about the "the economic tragedy of the twentieth century," the data they used to investigate that tragedy covers only 1960 to 2002. If the authors had stepped outside their own dataset, they could easily have found ways to figure out that "economic tragedy" is not an appropriate way to describe growth in African economies across the twentieth century. The problem is that scholars who depend on databases act as if anything that is outside their database does not exist.

Many studies of economic growth go further back. For example, some colonial statistical offices produced national account estimates as early as the late 1940s. One example is the rudimentary but official estimates that were made for Rhodesia and Nyasaland starting in 1945. In addition, many scholars have provided estimates for parts of the colonial period (e.g., Okigbo, 1962; Szereszewski, 1965; Deane, 1953; Bigsten, 1986). Finally, studies of economic growth do not have to be quantitative or based on a comparative database of complete national accounts. Arguments about economic growth can be made using partial or circumstantial evidence. Historical estimates of national accounts are based on partial records. These estimates cannot be fully assembled according to the requirements of the System of National Accounts and are made using assumptions to make up for missing data. Because of this, it is essential to have two ideas in one's head at the same time. First, the different kinds of estimates that we have do not tell us everything about economic development Africa and any new estimates will not provide us with the final word on growth. The information is partial and is open to interpretation. Second, despite their limitations, the new time-series data my colleagues and I have compiled changes what we thought we knew about African economic development. A lot of the economic history written by econometricians has been limited by the available time-series data. Early exchanges on economic development in Africa were about whether the visible growth in terms of known trade volumes and documented agrarian and industrial transformations meant that "development" had taken place or whether that data indicated "uneven development" in the leftist sense of that concept, where the periphery engages with the capitalist world economy in such a way that development of a capitalist economy is halted. Walter Rodney (1972) made the classic pessimistic leftist statement of this idea and John Sender and Sheila Smith made the argument in the classic, more optimistic Marxist interpretation (see review in Akram-Lodhi, 1988). Debates have specifically addressed the extent to which the growth in volume of agricultural exports coincided with growth, stagnation, or decline in the nonvisible sectors. Thus, questions of growth cannot be answered by historical national accounts drawn from the colonial ledgers alone. Those sources must be carefully considered in the context of a broader assessment of both the historical evidence and theoretical insights from competing models of agrarian change (Austin, 2014; Tosh, 1980).

I now turn to the prevailing wisdom on historical patterns of growth in Africa. Until quite recently, the dataset that provided the longest time series was Angus Maddison's historical statistics of the world economy (2009).[1]

Gareth Austin recommends caution when approaching these observations, reminding us that the literal interpretation of the word *data* is "things that are given" and that many of the historical income or population estimates used in the literature for African economies

Table 3.1 *African and world GDP per capita, selected years, 1* CE–*1950*

	1	1000	1500	1600	1700	1820	1870	1900	1913	1940	1950
Total Africa	472	425	414	422	421	420	500	601	637	813	889
World	467	453	566	596	615	667	871	1,262	1,525	1,958	2,109

Source: Maddison (2009). All values in constant 1990 International Geary-Khamis dollars. Note that the only African countries for which Maddison has individual income estimates during this period are Algeria, Egypt, Libya, Tunisia, and Morocco.

should therefore not be considered as data in the strictest sense (Austin, 2008). In Maddison's dataset, the underlying primary sources are not always available, but presumably the data before 1960 are projections that rely on proxy variables such as exports and taxation. (Annual national income estimates were generally not published before the 1960s.[2]) While annual international comparable GDP per capita "data" for all African countries are available only for the period 1950 to 2006, there are observations for the whole continent back to Year 1.

The GDP per capita estimates in Table 3.1 assume that on average "Africa" was richer than other parts of the world in Year 1. This is driven by an estimated higher income in Egypt than elsewhere in the world. The data implies that "Africa" gradually fell behind the rest of the world due to stagnation in income per capita from 1000 to 1820. From 1820 to 1913, income per capita increased in "Africa" but was falling further behind the world average as incomes increased more rapidly in other places. In the period 1913 to 1950, Africa stopped falling behind the world average, according to the data. In this period, the annual average GDP per capita growth was given as 1 percent without annual observations. Maddison estimates population growth (using data from the same dataset) to be 1 percent, meaning that the economies in Africa were growing at an average of 2 percent in this period.

In "African growth recurring" (Jerven 2010b), I argued that the general aggregate picture shown in Table 3.1 does not reflect what is known about periods of export growth, state formation, and accumulation in parts of Africa. There were large flows of factors of production and commodities, both internally and externally, during the Atlantic slave trade and the cash-crop revolution. Kingdoms rose and fell, colonial empires were established, and railways and mines were developed during this long period, yet the GDP per capita measure barely blinks. David Bloom and colleagues used an earlier version of the Maddison data to conclude that for the past two centuries, "Africa's poor economic growth has been chronic rather than episodic" (Bloom et al., 1998: 2). I argued that it is certain that well-documented growth in African markets for currency, labor, and goods led to Smithian growth through specialization in some areas (Jerven, 2010b). Moreover, the Atlantic trade brought not only exchange of commodities but also new technology – for instance, the introduction of new cultivars that must have led to an increase in total factor productivity (Austin, 2008: 588). In addition, economic growth could not have occurred without significant investments in improvements to the land, the planting of perennial crops, and growth in transport infrastructure. Finally, these growth episodes induced historically documented institutional changes such as the formation of markets for land and labor, the strengthening of states, and an increase in living standards. If we supplement the existing international databases (such as Maddison, 2009) with other evidence of economic growth and partial estimates of historical national accounts, it becomes apparent that historical growth in Africa is best approached as recurring rather than as permanently stagnant (Jerven 2010b). Since then quite a lot of scholarly attention has focused on extending the time series on economic change before 1960, so it is no longer necessary to take 1960 as Year 1 in the history of African economic growth.

Attempts to Increase the Time Span of the Database

Measuring GDP is notoriously difficult even today, especially in developing countries and sub-Saharan Africa. This is due to many reasons that include a country's statistical capacity, and of course how to fit the System of National Accounts to the statistical sources that are available to us now. The recent rebasing of GDP baselines in several African countries illustrates the challenge. For instance, rebasing in Ghana in 2010 resulted in a 60 percent increase in GDP. Similar results became evident in 2014 in Zambia and Nigeria, where rebasing resulted in an increase in GDP of 25 percent and 90 percent, respectively (Jerven, 2016a). Thus, getting the levels right is difficult. When we venture back in time where data points and records are quite scarce, it is not surprising that reliable GDP figures are hard to find. When we investigate the date in some of the largest databases (such as the Penn World Table or the Maddison dataset), we often find that these numbers are not as clear or reliable as they might appear to be (Jerven, 2014a).[3] There has been a growing awareness of this problem, and some have attempted to complement the data that is currently available. Lately, economic historians have begun to visit the older historical data on economic development in Africa before 1950. For other regions, greater access to data has made it easier to compile more databases of economic development over time (Jerven, 2012). But for sub-Saharan Africa (excluding South Africa), the data for such an approach is not yet available (Prados de la Escosura, 2012: 1).

The data for calculating GDP for African countries before 1950 is scarce. Traditional methods of summarizing growth for the period from the end of the nineteenth century to the mid-twentieth century involved various forms of calculations based on benchmark years, assumptions, and proxies. Although all models and calculations will be imperfect, the task at hand is to improve both the figures we have about growth and development in sub-Saharan Africa and our understanding of that data. This is about more than just getting the numbers right, it is just as much a question of understanding possible paths of development and whether these new portrayals of African economic growth suggest a different evaluation of Africa's recent economic past.

What follows is a short review of three recent approaches to understanding and measuring growth and GDP. They are quite distinct. The first, Smits et al. (2009) "A dataset on comparative historical accounts, ca 1870–1950: A time-series perspective," follows the established method of compiling historical national accounts. The other two provide more general datasets that were compiled with a new methodology that could prove useful for future research in sub-Saharan Africa: Prados de la Escosura (2012) offers an alternative to the conventional way of measuring growth in Africa that challenges some established truths, and Fariss et al. (2017) have written a paper that examines historic documents and other contemporary sources to arrive at "latent estimates" of GDP, GDP per capita, and population.

Smits, Woltjer, and Ma and the Groeningen Growth and Development Centre (GGDC) draw on more in-depth country information to increase the accuracy and validity of their dataset, which covers the period 1870–1950. Smits et al. (2009: 2–3) are not satisfied with crude GDP figures because they give little or no information about structural changes in an economy. The aim of their dataset is to break down GDP figures into a far more fine-grained sector-based data and from there fill in the missing data points. Their main focus is on the period 1870–1950, although they provide time series that go even further back in some cases. The major obstacle for the period after 1950 is differences in methodology based on the version of the System of National Accounts different countries used, which makes cross-country comparison difficult. The main focus of the GGDC dataset is the period up to 1950; it builds on existing data from the Madison dataset and supplements that with national records. The methodology in the estimates varies slightly from country to country, but generally Smits, Woltjer, and Ma rely on estimates based on imports or exports of various products that they have grouped and have assumed to be representative of activity in a larger sector. These data are not flawless for the purpose of cross-country comparison, as they suffer from changes in relative prices between countries and from changes in output and input relations.

The GGDC dataset also contains a line model between agricultural and industrial sectors from 1870 to the present day, but because of problems associated with various revisions in the System of National Accounts (and hence different ways of calculating GDP), the database provides these figures only in absolute levels. The authors argue that this will highlight trends even if direct cross-country comparison is not possible (Smits et al., 2009: 6). In the dataset, the timespan and methodology of national accounts vary and data sources are not clearly documented. There are plans to add to the dataset as more data becomes available and to develop the methodology further. This project and the database have not yet been formally published. The authors note that having a PPP benchmark adjustment that stretches over a long period of time is a challenge because countries, sectors, and the weight of products will vary across time. For instance, the common use of 1990 Geary-Khamis dollars (as in the Penn World Table and the Maddison dataset, among others) can be problematic, as that metric is built on relative strength based on a modern basket of goods that might not reflect a similar exercise 100 years earlier simply because the relative importance and value of the goods would be different.

Leandro Prados de la Escosura (2012) provides a different approach to calculating GDP in pre-independence Africa. He notes that GDP figures and data for Africa are notoriously unreliable, especially in the pre-independence era, and that a new approach to providing estimates is needed. Using foreign trade data as a proxy for growth, he presents new methods of calculating output and uses the resulting data as a proxy for growth figures (or GDP growth). His goal is to "draw explicit quantitative conjectures on long-run trends in real output per head on the basis of international trade data" (Prados de la Escosura, 2012: 2). He does this using two methods, both of which estimate GDP indirectly. The first model, which he calls the dual-economy approach, assumes no increase in GDP per head outside the tradable sector and accepts the purchasing power of exports as the proxy. This model builds on Szereszewski's (1965) concept of a dual economy, in which the "traditional" economy follows the population growth rate set to a fixed proportion of the tradable economy and the "modern" economy follows the growth rate of international trade.[4] As Prados de la Escosura notes, the major objection to this model is that it assumes no elasticity in price or demand for the goods in the nontradable sector. It also assumes that all growth takes place in the tradable sector. There is no reason to assume that growth will occur only in the (international) tradable sector.

Because of these limitations, Prados de la Escosura explores a related adaptation that he calls the "econometric approach." It follows much of the same logic as the dual-economy approach but uses an association between per capita GDP and the income terms of trade per capita plus various other control variables. It is worth nothing that this model assumes that the econometric relationship derived from 1950 to 1990 remains stable over time and can be transferred back to the period before 1950. This is quite an arbitrary solution that is difficult to assess empirically. Because these approaches refer to growth in per capita terms, they are subject to the same weakness as all other models of this kind: We lack both reliable growth figures and reliable population data for this period. Prados de la Escosura (2012) admits that this is a serious shortcoming, noting that Patrick Manning (2010) suggests that the population data for 1950 is generally overestimated. Ewout Frankema and I (2012) have challenged this assumption, arguing that using the Indian population data as Manning did to estimate historical population growth might not be a good fit for the African continent.

There is still no consensus on population data, and even relatively small changes in this factor would have a significant effect on the outcome of calculating GDP or growth per capita.

In addition to the two-measurements approach, Prados de la Escosura compared welfare ratios as derived from the data Frankema and van Waijenburg (2012) compiled, which had been based on an estimate of Geary-Khamis 1990 $300 as the level of absolute poverty. There are two reasons for adding this line to the data. First, it illustrates that generally speaking, Africa was well above this level for most of the colonial period. Furthermore, in British Africa, the difference between returns to raw labor (captured by the welfare ratio) and returns to all factors captured by GDP (or, in this case, Prados de la Escosura's proxy modeling of it) are relatively small, indicating that inequality was relatively low, although the gap seems to have increased between the eve of World War I and the Great Depression (Prados de la Escosura, 2012: 15). A second finding is a slight positive association between urbanization and output per capita, which is expected as these areas generally were the center of much economic activity and expansion of market through innovation (17).

In his summary of the long-run trends for Africa and sub-Saharan Africa, Prados de la Escosura found that the new estimates

... revise downwards Maddison's long-run growth for Africa, while increasing the level of income per head during the colonial period. Interestingly, neither the "dual" nor the "econometric" approach supports Maddison's contention that Africa was close to minimum subsistence levels (1990 Geary-Khamis $400). (Prados de la Escosura, 2012: 21–22)

The overall picture Prados de la Escosura presents is that growth started earlier than has previously been assumed and largely continued through the colonial period. Although there was a setback after World War I, growth resumed in the 1930s and 1940s. After that, Africa experienced a golden age of growth from 1950 to 1975. Furthermore, these conjectures grounded in quantitative evidence support the statement that growth can be traced back to 1900, contradicting the established view that African economies were characterized by stagnation during this era (Prados de la Escosura, 2012: 22–23).

The approach of Fariss et al. (2017) differs from the other projects in terms of both the range and the quality of the data. It builds on a range of existing datasets and covers the period 1500 CE to 2015 CE. This model is still subject to the general objections to and challenges of calculating GDP, but by relying on a multitude of sources and, most importantly, by keeping the model open in what they call a "latent model," they allow for the addition of both quantitative and qualitative data. This could be done by adding larger datasets or by adding a specific country case to the model, as I demonstrated with the use of my data on Ghana (Gold Coast) (Jerven 2014b). The new data then revises the original data and enhances our understanding of what the database tells us. This latent model is as much a platform for incorporating further research as it is a static dataset. The major advantage of this dataset is that it relies on a multitude of sources and provides a score of the quality of the data it projects. Finally, Fariss and colleagues provide all available metadata about the methods they used in the model for various years or cases, ensuring transparency. In addition to being a hybrid or combined model, the openness and the fact that the dataset doubles as a research tool are welcome advances in the way these databases are constructed.

Even though initiatives such as Fariss and colleagues' latent model should be applauded for its combination of several types of sources and for providing a quality score for the data, one must still bear in mind that no model is better than the data it builds on. Even when strides are made to overcome deficits in the data, they cannot be fully overcome. This is not a fault in the latent model, but it serves as an important reminder that even a complex model that relies on some of the largest datasets is incomplete and when new data are added or made available, the results might change.

To conclude, several recent ventures demonstrate how we can advance both our quantifiable knowledge of African economies and our understanding of African economic development. Two approaches offer a toolbox approach to researchers and scholars. The GGCD database provides an interesting approach to how sectors can and perhaps should be measured and raise interesting questions about how we calculate relative strength and compare units. This database's sectoral approach and its reminder that the relative weight of sectors and commodities vary over time provide new dimensions to our understanding of development.

The latent model in Fariss et al. (2017) is perhaps one of the most intellectually intriguing because it includes data from a range of sources and provides transparency about data sources. It is also a platform for further expansion as data becomes available. Its true strength is that it can be used both in association with larger quantitative datasets or with data from a country-specific analysis.

Prados de la Escosura (2012) uses international trade data as a proxy for GDP and ties this metric proportionally to the domestic sector. Through two slightly different models, he shows how economic growth in sub-Saharan Africa began earlier and continued more consistently than had been assumed, and that there are strong linkages between growth in the colonial era and the pre-independence period.

These are interesting approaches that inspire, provide a foundation for new work, or offer new interpretations. However, despite growing attention to the issue of African growth before 1960 and new initiatives, there is still a need for a more comprehensive and accurate way to measure economic development in sub-Saharan Africa. This is not only a numbers game but also a way of understanding domestic policies and development that are easily lost in large regression models that rely on a few data points.

Prospects for Estimating GDP Using Historical Data

Our knowledge of economic change based on the state records in colonial and postcolonial Africa is limited. I have argued elsewhere that because of measurement problems and contradictory data, the most prudent course of action might be to plead ignorance regarding population growth and agricultural productivity (Jerven, 2013). This limitation has far-reaching implications. It means that the most important indicators for assessing the evolution in living standards are missing. It also implies that any level estimates of per capita income are futile and probably grossly misleading.[5]

Therefore, I suggest that since there are fairly reliable data on exports, imports, and government expenditures and revenue for the whole period, the best option for quantitative analysis is to create a consistent dataset of these measures across the twentieth century. I am suggesting a measure of the rate of change in formal markets. The advantage of this method is that it explicitly takes the data limitations into consideration. The information in the first part of this chapter suggests that per capita income, the conventional indicator of development, is unreliable and unsuitable for pre-independence Africa. Any level estimate would be subject to a range of obscure assumptions. In addition, the data basis for the level estimates is changed over time, thereby biasing the change estimates.

In the available official GDP estimates published by governments or in international datasets, only the information on government expenditures, large commercial firms, and imports and exports is available and reliable. The rest of the data are subject to assumptions and ad hoc measures. These published estimates lack transparency about what these assumptions are, whether they changed over time, and whether they were consistent from country to country. In addition, the informal economy is largely unrecorded. While there are many misnomers for this sector, such as "subsistence economy" or "traditional economy," the best definition of this economic activity is that it is not recorded and thus is not taxed or otherwise monitored by the state. Unrecorded does not mean unimportant or insignificant for historical arguments about economic change.

In the estimation method I am suggesting here, this important part of the economy will be treated as an unknown quantity. What can data on exports, imports, and government expenditures and revenue tell us about development? It is probably best conceived as a measure of a state's capacity to capture economic rents and the ability of producers to participate in external markets. Thus, the first useful outcome for future studies in African economic history is an overview of the availability of consistent time-series data. Of course, it is not immediately obvious that the issues I am highlighting here are directly relevant to all other African countries, but some of the features of the data weaknesses are recurring. The second goal is to illustrate the type of bare-bone growth estimates that can be created from rather limited data observations. I have devised this method to rely as far as possible only on recorded growth and to minimize assumptions while making them as transparent as possible.

The weakest part of the estimation is that growth occurs from growth in formal markets, and we are not certain of the opportunity cost of growth in such markets. How should the relationship between the formal or recorded sectors of the economy be interpreted? Addressing this issue for Nigeria in 1966, Stolper (2014: 21) wrote, "The absence of a Malthusian problem makes it illegitimate to neglect the so-called subsistence sector and to assume that any increase in output by 'modern' sectors is a net addition to total product." Is this claim valid? For the whole period? It is precisely these questions that need to be addressed before we can interpret the figures that express formal, recorded, or "modern" economic growth in Nigeria or elsewhere. Although household budget surveys, which give a fairly reliable estimate of the level of consumption, are available for more recent times, changes in production patterns are a matter of guesswork.

Thus, these measured changes in the formal economy need to be complemented by qualitative analysis. The economic history, development, and anthropology literatures have typically focused on two relationships. One is the relationship between growth in exports or the modern sector and how this related to change in the unobserved economy. There is not room to do the whole of the literature justice, but I outline some of the most important arguments relating to particular times and areas here. In particular, the literature has examined the extent to which classic economic models apply, such as vent for surplus and/or unlimited supply of labor. These debates are directly relevant because they explicitly or implicitly discuss whether the assumption of an unlimited supply of labor is accurate, and thus whether rural marginal productivity approached zero or whether the opportunity cost of export growth was close to zero, as in the vent-for-surplus model.

In *Economic Change in Precolonial Africa* (1975), a monograph that marshaled an impressive amount of quantitative evidence to analyze the precolonial economic history of Senegambia, Philip D. Curtin does not discuss external trade until the final chapter. This was a deliberate choice:

External trade usually comes first in writing about African economic history, mainly because the historiographic tradition was laid down by Europeans who first saw Africa through the commerce that linked the two societies. This time it has been left till last. (Curtin, 1975: 309)

He did this in order to maintain a Senegambian perspective and because he argues that this is the appropriate order of importance and analysis. Only a small part of territorial gross product entered external trade, and it only makes sense to analyze these trade flows and their relative importance after the domestic conditions for production of export commodities and the slave trade have been discussed in detail.

Also in 1975, Patrick Manning reviewed an economic history of Nigeria written by Olufemi Ekundare that focused almost exclusively on external trade. Manning wrote that the book was valuable only as a "compendium of official data on British intervention in the Nigerian economy" and that the accompanying analysis was a "celebratory narrative" of that intervention. He concluded that "the only interpretative lines drawn out of the data presented are the assertion that the British government was the main stimulant of Nigerian economic growth" (1975: 315). This should suffice to make it clear that writing an account of economic growth based on external trade statistics alone risks certain pitfalls.

Yet that is roughly what this chapter sets out to do. The justification is that in the past ten years there has been a surge in quantitative research on African development that attempts to establish relationships between historical events and income levels and inequalities today (for reviews, see Austin, 2008; and Hopkins, 2009). To date, the quantitative literature on Africa has made heroic leaps of faith that assert causal relationships across time periods even though it is not possible to account for different trajectories of economic development. One basic reason is that data on national income are available only back to 1950.[6]

Elsewhere I have argued that the result is that we have a literature that focuses on explaining present-day outcomes such as observable income differentials and that to enrich these perspectives we should focus on explaining African economic growth instead of explaining the lack of it (Jerven, 2011a, 2010b). For this research agenda to be fruitful and for its theories to be substantiated, it is crucial to have consistent and reliable estimates of economic change. The sources for the creation of long-term datasets on African economies exist, but valuable colonial-era data remains underutilized. Meanwhile, historical national accounts that stretch far back in time are currently being constructed for European countries and other regions (Jerven, 2012).[7] If Africa is not to be marginalized in global economic studies, similar reconstructive research should be undertaken where it is feasible. The use of these quantitative and other indicators must further be enriched by qualitative studies of the dynamics between formal economic growth and informal economic growth. This section presents some preliminary estimates of economic growth for a set of former British colonies: The Gambia, Ghana, Nigeria, Kenya, Tanzania, Uganda, Sierra Leone, and Malawi.[8] Before doing so, I situate the growth estimates in the literature on the expansion of world trade and the economic development of Africa, which allows us to evaluate some supporting evidence of growth and development in the early twentieth century.

The issue of world trade and African economic development in the nineteenth and twentieth centuries has been much discussed and analyzed. Although economic historians have documented some aspects of them very well, our knowledge of the relationship between trade and development is not evenly distributed. Three points are worth making. First, we know more about world trade than we know about how it affected participating countries. Second, we know more about how it affected the core economies than how it affected peripheral economies. Finally, in the periphery, we know less about how it affected sub-Saharan African economies.[9] In summary, we are in good position to pinpoint changes in the explanatory variable – be it in trade volumes, prices, or values – while we have a paucity of observations relating to GDP, wages, poverty, population, and other data about living standards in the periphery. This is particularly true for sub-Saharan Africa.

As Jeffery Williamson (2011) has recently documented, during the "first global century," or from 1820 to 1913, there was a big boom in world trade that featured some year-to-year volatility and heterogeneity at the country level. This created a terms-of-trade boom for the periphery.[10] Strong income growth in the core economies is well documented in this period; hence we speak of the "great divergence." The question comes down to whether peripheral economies failed to benefit and if so, why. Because the main characteristic that distinguishes the two types of economies is the structure of exports, another way of putting it is whether primary commodity exports failed to offer the same benefits as exports of manufactured goods.

Williamson investigates three hypotheses: (1) Whether the trade boom caused a deindustrialization in the periphery; (2) whether the trade boom caused income inequality in the periphery; and (3) whether export specialization increased income volatility. Williamson (2011: 28) does not include Africa in his investigation because data on Africa are missing, but presents evidence for the rest of the periphery. He finds that the "third world" did make gains from the world boom in trade. More specifically, trade did increase income levels but was associated with some deindustrialization and considerable increased volatility following the specialization in production of primary products for exports.

How does Africa fit into this picture? Because of the paucity of quantitative evidence that pinpoints shifts in income and living standards, the literature has been a contest of models and plausible assumptions. It can be boiled down to three competing perspectives: The classical and neoclassical gain-from-trade perspective, the dependency and new left core-periphery-exploitation perspective, and the political economy "cui bono?" perspective, in which both old and new Marxists and rational choice theorists emphasize the importance of who stood to gain rather than on whether growth really represents gains from trade or merely records the fruits of exploitation.

The basic competing models are vent-for-surplus and dependency. The former assumes that there was a surplus of factors of production, particularly labor and land, and that the world market provided a vent for these abundant factors of production. Thus, when we see increased export volumes, the opportunity cost is zero. This model assumes that a marginal productivity of labor is zero in the "traditional" or "rural" economies, as does the classical dual-economy model Arthur Lewis proposed. The main distinction is that in the Lewis model, land was assumed to be the constraining factor, and thus the opportunity cost of modern-sector growth (here manufacturing and industry instead of agriculture) was also zero. In the vent-for-surplus model, both land and labor are abundant and the modern-sector growth (here export instead of food) is assumed to be zero. In different ways, scholarship has contested these assumptions or explanations. Most important, it has been pointed out that labor was only seasonally abundant and was very scarce in certain periods (and more so in more areas outside the forest belt), that producing exports involved both innovation and capital (investment in new technologies), and that the opportunity costs were not zero (food quality and security, division of labor, and manufacturing all changed considerably).[11] These and other empirical contributions remind us that when we see aggregate modern-sector growth, it is not equivalent to aggregate economic growth.

Other scholars not only take issue with the assumptions, but also analyze the political economy of growth. They point out that the move from "traditional" to "modern" was fundamentally driven by power. The colonial state was interested in increasing taxable activities and increasing labor supply and thus had an incentive to undermine food production and promote export production. It did so by introducing taxes or alienating land in various degrees across the continent.[12] These revisions make the point that when we see aggregate modern-sector growth, it is not tantamount to "development" and that we should focus on who benefits from this particular type of economic growth.

Trade and Growth: What Numbers Do We Have?

Thus, there are some very powerful caveats to the interpretation of aggregate data trends. However, the literature leaves no doubt: there must have been economic growth. A lot of this growth was extensive and happened by applying more factors of production, but there was also intensive growth. There was Smithian growth through specialization and Schumpeterian growth as entrepreneurs adapted new technologies and invested capital. However, Hopkins (1973) reminds us that while there was economic growth, it was limited, chiefly because exports were confined to staples and the import side was dominated by consumer goods. Thus, opportunities for spurring economic growth were limited on both sides. Furthermore, income inequality prohibited the formation of a mass consumer market and the total proceeds from exports were too small to support the formation of a wide range of enterprises on the continent. As Kilby's (1969: 54) calculations bear out, the domestic market in Nigeria was not able to support basic light manufacturing industries until the 1950s.[13]

Munro (1976) provided a useful study of Africa and the international economy from 1800 to 1960. His aim was simply to provide an account of broad trends and patterns in the development of sub-Saharan Africa and to provide a foundation for further study. He then provided a collection of aggregate trade statistics but did not test or apply any theories of development. That kind of contribution is very important because aggregate statistics enable us to compare across the periphery and gauge the importance of the different constraints that have been discussed here (see Table 3.2).

The aggregate growth in foreign trade is far less impressive when it is expressed in constant prices. Table 3.3 shows the same data for all of Africa expressed in fixed 1913 British pounds using an average of Feinstein's import and export deflator (1972, Table 61). The Growth row is the annual average growth for each of the periods. The average growth in foreign trade from 1897 to 1960 was 3.64 percent, but this growth was unevenly distributed. Large gains were made until World War I, but then were almost entirely reversed after the war. Although

Table 3.2 *Total foreign trade, Africa, selected years, 1897–1960 (in millions of British pounds)*

	Africa	West Africa	Central Africa	Southern Africa	Eastern Africa
1897	71.1	10.1	4.1	52.2	4.6
1913	187.9	41.3	10.1	121.6	14.9
1919	274.4	63.5	14.8	168.8	27.4
1929	355.7	83.3	28.7	201.3	42.3
1932	204.4	47.6	16.6	117.8	22.3
1938	391.7	73.2	26.6	248.6	43.3
1945	603.4	118.1	56.6	347.8	80.9
1952	2789.2	725.2	412.0	1238.3	413.7
1960	3782.2	1089.3	457.9	1725.4	509.7

Source: Munro (1976: Appendix).

Table 3.3 *Total foreign trade, Africa, 1897–1960*

	1897	1913	1919	1929	1932	1938	1945	1952	1960
Trade	87.6	187.9	106.2	272.4	197.1	327.5	260.8	606	834.9
Growth (%)		4.8	–9.1	9.9	–10.2	8.8	–3.2	12.8	4.1

Source: Munro (1976: Appendix).

annual growth was impressive from 1919 to 1929, the rate of decline was in double digits for three years during the Great Depression. After World War II, growth was the fastest in foreign trade recorded in the whole period.

We know less about African GDP estimates for this period. As mentioned, Maddison provides the few GDP per capita estimates that exist, including country estimates for all of Africa, for South Africa, and for the northern African economies, but only for Ghana among the sub-Saharan economies (see Table 3.4).

These data indicate that Ghana was growing exceptionally rapidly in the period 1870 to 1960. Its GDP per capita in the period 1870–1913 almost doubled and then almost doubled again in the period 1913–1960. According to these data, Ghana's economy grew at a rate roughly double the pace of total Africa and almost 25 percent faster

Table 3.4 *Selected per capita GDP estimates, selected years, 1820–1960 (in 1990 international Geary-Khamis dollars)*

	Africa	World	UK	Ghana	South Africa	Brazil	India	Japan
1820	420	666	1,706	415	415	646	533	669
1870	500	870	3,190	439	858	713	533	737
1913	637	1524	4,921	781	1602	811	673	1387
1960	1063	2773	8,645	1378	3041	1,702	662	3986

Source: Maddison 2009.

than the world average. The selected countries from the periphery (or semi-periphery) did not show similar growth. The only exception is Japan, which kept pace with Ghana from 1870 to 1913, but then Ghana outpaced Japan from 1913 to 1960. Recent annual estimates for the Gold Coast from 1890 to 1954 reaffirm this growth rate and indicate that it may also have been growing faster than indicated by Maddison's estimates (Jerven 2011c). Moreover, the average slow growth from 1870 to 1960 is misleading; Jerven (2011c) shows that annual growth rates are much more volatile, as the more episodic growth rates in foreign trade shown in Table 3.3 display.

Three questions arise. First, how does Ghana compare with other African economies? Second, how certain are we about these GDP estimates for Ghana? And third, how do these estimates cohere with other data from the same period? I will deal with these questions in what follows.

Frankema and van Waijenburg (2011) have collected price and wage data from the colonial blue books to give us a picture of economic development in British colonial Africa through wage developments. The nominal wages are summarized in table 3.5.

The picture in nominal wages does not immediately cohere with the GDP estimates. First, we only have wage data from 1880 onward, but on the other hand we do have wage data for more countries. It is striking that while GDP increased 78 percent in the Gold Coast from 1870 to 1913, nominal wages only increased 22 percent from 1880 to 1913. From 1913 to 1960, GDP increased another 76 percent, but wages increased 343 percent. Of course, most of the work with nominal wages is done through prices. In

Table 3.5 *Nominal wages in Gold Coast, Sierra Leone, Kenya, Nyasaland, Tanganyika, and Uganda (minus South Africa), selected years, 1880–1959 (in British pence per day)*

	Gold Coast	Sierra Leone	Kenya	Nyasaland	Tanganyika	Uganda
1880	10.4	10.8	—	—	—	—
1890	10.4	10.9	—	—	—	—
1900	10.4	10	—	—	—	—
1915	12.7	10	4.3	3.3	—	4.8
1930	15	13.9	7.1	4.2	8.9	9.9
1945	22	20.8	15	5.7	6.2	9.2
1951	34.5	40.2	28.4	16.1	25.5	16.8
1959	56.3	80.4	55.2	21	32.8	29.2

Source: Frankema and van Waijenburg (2011: Appendix, Table 1a).

Table 3.6 *Deflated wages in Gold Coast, Sierra Leone, Kenya, Nyasaland, Tanganyika, and Uganda, selected years, 1880–1959 (selected years) (in 1913 British pence per day)*

	Gold Coast	Sierra Leone	Kenya	Nyasaland	Tanganyika	Uganda
1880	11.0	11.4	—	—	—	—
1890	11.6	12.2	—	—	—	—
1900	11.0	10.6	—	—	—	—
1915	11.4	9.0	3.9	3.0	—	4.3
1930	8.6	8.0	4.1	2.4	5.1	5.7
1945	8.3	7.9	5.7	2.2	2.4	3.5
1951	9.9	11.5	8.1	4.6	7.3	4.8
1959	11.5	16.5	11.3	4.3	6.7	6.0

Source: Frankema and van Waijenburg (2011: Appendix, Table 1a) and my calculations.

Table 3.6, the wages are deflated using the GDP deflator from Feinstein (1976: Table 61).

When wages are deflated, it seems clear that if there was GDP growth in the Gold Coast it was not benefiting urban unskilled workers. The only colony where wages were increasing was in Kenya. Note that while most of this increase occurred from 1945 to 1959, this finding is counterintuitive. According to the Lewis model (as clearly laid out in

Mosley, 1963; and Bowden et al., 2008) we would expect the wages of urban unskilled workers to be lower there because land supply was constrained as part of the polices of a settler economy. The differences in levels (between West Africa and East and South Africa) seem to cohere, but the trend in Kenya does not. However, in order to compare wages across countries confidently, it is not enough to deflate by currency: The wages should be expressed in purchasing power parity.

Frankema and van Waijenburg (2011) provide an attempt to do this. They adopted Allen's (2009) subsistence basket methodology and collected urban retail prices to calculate the annual price of a family subsistence basket. They then used this data to create a measure of comparison, namely how many days one urban skilled worker would have to work to finance one family. Tables 3.7 and 3.8 show that the data needed to compile the baskets are not available for all benchmark years, and Frankema and van Waijenburg further note that some observations are not urban retail prices but are instead import prices with a 20 percent markup. Note that Nyasaland is an outlier, not because of price levels but because of low nominal wages.

The deflation of real wages by the cost of the subsistence basket shows that the currency deflation understated welfare gains among urban wage earners in the Gold Coast and elsewhere (see Table 3.9). How did these trends cohere with what we know of export, imports,

Table 3.7 *Cost of subsistence baskets in Gold Coast, Sierra Leone, Kenya, Nyasaland, Tanganyika, and Uganda, 1880–1959 (selected years) (in British pence per year)*

	Gold Coast	Sierra Leone	Kenya	Nyasaland	Tanganyika	Uganda
1880	596.7	722	—	—	—	—
1890	529.4	642.1	—	—	—	—
1900	484.3	—	—	—	—	—
1915	—	1,051.2	492	455.2	—	537.2
1930	453.4	982.6	527.3	578.1	507.2	832.2
1945	803.7	1,434.6	982.0	—	902.7	873.7
1951	1,370.9	2,090.6	1,831.5	—	1,751.2	1,282.7
1959	1,459.0	2,742.0	27,80.4	1,746.0	2,136.4	1,437.8

Source: Frankema and van Waijenburg (2011, Appendix, Table 1b).

Table 3.8 *Days of work required to earn enough to purchase a subsistence basket for a family in Gold Coast, Sierra Leone, Kenya, Nyasaland, Tanganyika, and Uganda, 1880–1959 (selected years)*

	Gold Coast	Sierra Leone	Kenya	Nyasaland	Tanganyika	Uganda
1880	57.4	66.9	—	—	—	—
1890	50.9	58.9	—	—	—	—
1900	46.6	—	—	—	—	—
1915	—	105.1	114.4	137.9	—	111.9
1930	30.2	70.7	74.3	137.6	57.0	84.1
1945	36.5	69.0	65.5	—	145.6	95.0
1951	39.7	52.0	64.5	—	68.7	76.4
1959	25.9	34.1	50.4	83.1	65.1	49.2

Source: Frankema and van Waijenburg (2011, Appendix, Tables 1a and 1b) and my calculations.

Table 3.9 *Real wages deflated by cost of subsistence basket in Gold Coast, Sierra Leone, Kenya, Nyasaland, Tanganyika, and Uganda (in 1930 British pence)*

	Gold Coast	Sierra Leone	Kenya	Nyasaland	Tanganyika	Uganda
1880	7.9	14.7	—	—	—	—
1890	8.9	16.7	—	—	—	—
1900	9.7	—	—	—	—	—
1915	—	9.3	4.6	4.2		7.4
1930	15.0	13.9	7.1	4.2	8.9	9.9
1945	12.4	14.2	8.1	—	3.5	8.8
1951	11.4	18.9	8.2	—	7.4	10.9
1959	17.5	28.8	10.5	7.0	7.8	16.9

Source: Frankema and van Waijenburg (2011, Appendix, Tables 1a and 1b) and my calculations.

and government expenditures and revenues? Frankema (2011) has provided an overview of colonial taxation and gives a comparative picture of the relationship between taxes and wages (see Table 3.10).

In essence, tables 3.10 and 3.11 capture different taxation systems. In particular, it is clear that in the Gambia, Sierra Leone, and the Gold Coast, revenue from custom duties were very important. Government

Table 3.10 *Days of work required to earn enough to have to pay the annual average per capita tax: Gambia, Sierra Leone, Gold Coast, Nigeria, Nyasaland, Kenya, Uganda, and Mauritius, 1910–1938*

	Gambia	Sierra Leone	Gold Coast	Nigeria	Nyasaland	Kenya	Uganda	Mauritius
1910–13	7.8	5.4	10.2	3.9	7.2	6.9	3.3	12.3
1919–21	6.5	4.5	12.7	3.1	12.1	–	6.1	12.4
1925	9.5	6.9	14.5	3.7	13.5	16.1	5.9	16.1
1929	8.7	6.8	13.0	2.6	13.3	21.8	9.1	14.2
1934	–	5.4	11.4	3.8	10.4	18.2	11.8*	26.8
1938	9.7	9.2	14.4	4.7	12.6	23.3	14.5	28.4

Source: Frankema (2011: 141, Table 1). *Data from 1933.

Table 3.11 *Days of work required to earn enough to have to pay the per capita tax, excluding custom duties: Gambia, Sierra Leone, Gold Coast, Nigeria, Nyasaland, Kenya, Uganda, and Mauritius, 1910–1938*

	Gambia	Sierra Leone	Gold Coast	Nigeria	Nyasaland	Kenya	Uganda	Mauritius
1910–13	1	1	1	1	5	5	3	6
1919–21	1	1	1	1	8	–	5	7
1925	2	1	1	1	10	9	4	7
1929	2	2	2	1	9	11	7	8
1934	–	2	2	1	6	11	8	15
1938	3	4	3	1	7	13	9	16

Source: Frankema (2011: 142: Table 2).

revenue and urban wages were higher in both real and nominal terms. Foreign trade for all of sub-Saharan Africa grew at the rate of 3.64 per annum from 1897 to 1960. Population estimates are not very reliable, but according to the Maddison dataset, growth in population averaged just short of 1.5 percent per annum from 1900 to 2000. Thus, throughout the continent, foreign trade grew at a rate of 2 percent per year. Between these two averages, there is wide spatial and temporal variation.

In addition to an uneven growth in trade, foreign trade decreased during the world wars and the Great Depression. World trade was more important in western Africa than it was in other areas. It has been observed that throughout the period, foreign trade was correlated with higher real wages and a relative higher importance of duties on trade for national revenue. According to the available data, annual GDP per capita growth in all of Africa was just above 0.5 percent from 1870 to 1913 and then just above 1.0 percent from 1913 to 1960. In the Gold Coast, GDP per capita grew faster than the average (1.35 percent from 1870 to 1913 and 1.2 percent 1913 to 1960). Was this growth distributed unequally among governments, wage earners, and exporters? These questions can be answered with respect to only a handful of British colonies.

Data for real wages, as measured by the changes in nominal wages paid to urban unskilled workers deflated by the price changes in the subsistence basket, show that incomes for urban wage earners in Accra increased marginally more slowly than estimated GDP growth until 1900, then grew at an annual rate of 1.45 percent from 1900 to 1930 (which was faster than GDP per capita growth). Note that this increase was not reflected in nominal prices, The average wage of 10.4 pence did not change from 1880 to 1900 (see Table 3.5) and then increased to only 12.7 in 1915 and 15 pence 1930. Deflated to 1913 British pounds as per Feinstein's index, the wages remained virtually unchanged from 1880 to 1960. Although they fell in the interwar period, for the rest of the period they behaved as if they were pegged to the British GDP deflator (Table 3.6). When domestic prices (or in some cases the prices of imported consumer goods) are added (as in Tables 3.12, working through the steps in tables 3.9–3.11), there is more movement in urban wages. If we trusted these data, we would conclude that the domestic price of subsistence decreased more rapidly in the Gold Coast than it did in Britain from 1880 to 1930 and therefore that urban unskilled workers experienced faster growth in real living standards. This trend is probably overstated, or rather misstated, because of the missing observation in 1915. In comparison, the data for Sierra Leone indicates negative growth in real wages for the period 1890–1915.

The general pattern seems to point toward growth across the board from 1915 to 1930. This change was not driven by increases in nominal wages, but real growth increased as the domestic price of the urban subsistence basket fell compared to the nominal wage. The average growth in foreign trade in this period was 9.9 percent (measured in constant prices). Real wage growth did not occur across the countries again until the postwar period, when it was again driven

Table 3.12 *Real wage growth, Gold Coast, Sierra Leone, Kenya, Nyasaland, Tanganyika, and Uganda, 1880–1959*

	Gold Coast	Sierra Leone	Kenya	Nyasaland	Tanganyika	Uganda
1880–1890	1.20	1.27	—	—	—	—
1890–1900	0.89	—	—	—	—	—
1900–1915	—	—	—	—	—	—
1915–1930	—	2.68	2.92	0.01	—	1.93
1930–1945	–1.26	0.16	0.84	—	–6.06	–0.81
1945–1951	–1.39	4.82	0.25	—	13.34	3.70
1951–1959	5.49	5.42	3.14	—	0.66	5.64

Source: Frankema and van Waijenburg (2011, Appendix, Table 1b) and my calculations. Gold Coast 1900–1930: +1.45; Sierra Leone 1890–1915: –2.29; Nyasaland 1930–1959: +1.75.

in part by increases in nominal wages (that this time were higher than the Feinstein GDP deflator for the period) and in part by a drop in the price of the subsistence basket. This positive development was underpinned by strong growth in foreign trade after 1945.

World Trade, Poverty, and Growth in Africa: New GDP Time Series Data

How close are we to saying something definite about GDP growth in the period? The data in the Maddison series have too few observations from too few countries. According to that dataset, the GDP per capita growth in Ghana averaged 1.35 percent from 1870 to 1913 and then slowed down to 1.2 percent from 1913 to 1960. The main cause for the slowdown was an increase in population growth, but we know that the population data are too weak to make this assertion. My alternative estimates (2011c), which adopt a version of Szereszewski's (1965) methods to estimate annual population increase from 1890 to 1954, show a slightly higher average annual growth. Table 3.13 shows a few annual observations. The estimates in my series show that GDP per capita grew more rapidly than the Maddison dataset indicates until 1913. Both 1920 and 1930 are odd years in the Jerven data series, reflecting that the tonnage of cocoa exports fell 30 percent in 1920 compared to the previous year, and 20 percent in 1930. The Jerven

Table 3.13 *Two estimates of GDP per capita for Ghana, selected years*

	1891	1900	1913	1920	1930	1940	1945	1950
Maddison	581	656	781	836	922	1,017	1,068	1,122
Jerven	581	639	833	646	778	989	1,040	1,311

Source: Total GDP growth from Jerven (2014b), using interpolations from Maddison's population data to create GDP per capita estimates. Maddison's year estimates are made using interpolated annual growth between his 1870, 1913 and 1950 estimates.

series picks up annual changes in physical exports, and thus there is more annual variation. Compared to the Maddison dataset, it shows more rapid growth before 1913, a more pronounced boom in the 1920s, a deep recession in the 1930s, similar growth into the World War II years, and stronger growth after the war.

To enrich the study of economic growth in colonial Africa, these time-series data can be expanded further. The basic components exist. We know a little bit about wages and population and less about production. We know considerably more about exports, imports, and government revenue and expenditures. Given this, compiling estimates will involve some deal of qualified guessing.

The underlying database for this project collects time-series data on imports, exports (quantities and values), government expenditures and revenue, wages, prices and a set of quantitative indicators (number of pupils enrolled, kilometers of road, kilowatt hours consumed, etc.). Data collection for Botswana, the Gambia, Ghana, Kenya, Malawi, Nigeria, Sierra Leone, Tanzania, Zambia, and Zimbabwe is ongoing. The colonial data has been collected using primarily the colonial blue books. Some gaps in the postcolonial data from national statistical offices still remain. A pilot study for constructing parsimonious national accounts based on physical indicators for Ghana has been completed for the years 1891 to 1954 (Jerven, 2011c), and the difficulties of creating a coherent dataset, focusing on the case of Nigeria, have been discussed at length (Jerven, 2018a). What follows are some preliminary estimates using data for the Gambia, the Gold Coast, Nigeria, Kenya, Tanganyika, Uganda, and Nyasaland.

According to the snapshot in Table 3.14, it seems that in 1931, revenues and expenditures in colonial Gambia, Gold Coast, and Kenya were as much as three to four times higher than those of

Table 3.14 *Colonial population (in thousands) and per capita estimates (in British pounds) for Gambia, Gold Coast, Nigeria, Kenya, Tanganyika, Uganda, and Nyasaland, 1931*

	Gambia	Gold Coast	Nigeria	Kenya	Tanganyika	Uganda	Nyasaland
Population	200	2,950	19,200	3,040	5,063	3,553	1,630
Revenue	0.92	0.77	0.25	0.72	0.30	0.39	0.27
Expenditure	1.14	0.96	0.32	1.01	0.35	0.41	0.31
Imports	1.26	1.63	0.34	1.89	0.84	0.37	0.46
Exports	2.58	2.57	0.45	1.48	0.84	0.56	0.31
G/X-M	0.5	0.4	0.7	0.5	0.4	0.9	0.8

Source: Colonial reports and blue books (various years), Kuczynski (1937) for population, and my calculations.

Uganda, Nyasaland, and Tanganyika. The ratios are similar for per capita exports and imports except in Tanganyika, where exports and imports were relatively high compared to the level of revenues and expenditures. The last row provides a measure of the role of the expansive nature of the colonial government. Basically, it is a measure of the share of the government as a ratio of the value of trade. Because we don't want to pick up arbitrary change in exports relative to import or revenue versus expenditure in any given year, I use the average value of imports–exports that year, and the average total of revenue and exports the same year. The average of per capita revenues and expenditures divided by the average of per capita imports and exports show that in Nigeria, Uganda, and Nyasaland, the size of government revenues and expenditures is close to total export earnings minus import expenditure, whereas in the Gambia, Gold Coast, and Kenya the share is about half that recorded in the other three countries. Again, as in comparing the levels of wages, these results can just as easily indicate different colonial government strategies rather than an expression of different levels of development. If we can create growth estimates of different components of GDP, the measures may shed light on this particular problem. Tables 3.15, 3.16, and 3.17 display selected years of total revenue, total government expenditures, and import and export data in fixed 1913 values (in thousands of British pounds).

The easiest way to compute GDP from these data is to use the expenditure method

Table 3.15 *Total government revenue for Gambia, Gold Coast, Nigeria, Kenya, Tanganyika, Uganda, and Nyasaland, selected years, 1895–1965 (in thousands of 1913 British pounds)*

	Gambia	Gold Coast	Nigeria	Kenya	Tanganyika	Uganda	Nyasaland
1895	30.6	269.1	166.1	—	—	—	—
1903	—	630.5	992.4	—	—	56.2	82.9
1914	86.3	1,335.7	2,948.8	979.0	—	283.7	118.9
1930	122.0	1,970.4	3,165.5	1,700.8	984.8	795.2	225.4
1950	—	5,842.9	9,168.0	3,702.5	2,906.6	3,085.5	767.2
1965	—	18,652.3	21,139.5	4,084.5	5,516.9	6,340.3	985.3

Source: Colonial reports and blue books (various years).

Table 3.16 *Total government expenditures for Gambia, Gold Coast, Nigeria, Kenya, Tanganyika, Uganda, and Nyasaland, selected years, 1895–1965 (in thousands of 1913 British pounds)*

	Gambia	Gold Coast	Nigeria	Kenya	Tanganyika	Uganda	Nyasaland
1895	29.3	310.3	168.4	—	—	—	—
1903	—	648.4	1,397.4	—	—	203.9	111.9
1914	121.3	1,761.1	3,606.8	848.6	—	290.1	143.6
1930	142.6	2,108.1	3,564.2	1,376.6	1033.2	795.2	241.5
1950	—	3,954.0	8,495.4	3495.6	2,272.0	2,236.6	1,005.9
1965	—	19,788.0	11,559.2	4,335.0	8,367.3	—	2,344.2

Source: Colonial reports and blue books (various years).

$$Y = C + I + G + [X - M]$$

where Y is total GDP, C is consumption, I is investment, G is government expenditure, X is value of exports, and M is value of imports. Previous estimates have used a base year with sector shares in GDP and let volume indices serve as a proxy for growth (Jerven, 2014b). The dataset has enough coverage of values and volumes of exports and imports for it to be possible to calculate income terms of trade. The same approach would let us create chain indices (changing weights each year) for imports and exports in both prices and volumes. In

Table 3.17 *Total imports for Gambia, Gold Coast, Nigeria, Kenya, Tanganyika, Uganda, and Nyasaland, selected years, 1896–1965 (in thousands of 1913 British pounds)*

	Gambia	Gold Coast	Nigeria	Kenya	Tanganyika	Uganda	Nyasaland
1895	—	961.3	—	—	—	—	—
1903	—	2,339.9	2,392.1	—	497.8	138.4	248.0
1914	384.1	4,408.5	6,208.7	1,453.2	—	582.5	200.6
1930	458.4	7,562.3	10,657.9	6,831.9	3,142.7	1,363.3	645.6
1950	962.7	14,107.3	18,190.5	8,869.3	7,107.6	4,619.9	2,228.7
1965	—	30,802.5	58,722.2	10,281.4	15,415.7	—	4,700.2

Source: Colonial reports and blue books (various years).

addition, either import price indices or consumer price indices can be used to complement existing GBP deflators to express revenues and expenditures in constant values.

The problematic entities are investment and consumption. The typical practice is to let population growth serve as a proxy for consumption, but that leaves open the question of guessing the right level. Is personal consumption 95 percent, 85 percent, 65 percent of total GDP, or less than that? How much of this consumption is accounted for by recorded imports and recorded urban retail prices? These assumptions will affect the pace of growth significantly. The assumption that traditional consumption grows with population growth assumes zero elasticity between the two sectors, whereas we would expect that consumers, wage earners, and export producers actively engage in both sectors, as our models of the relationship between export and development rightly assume. As economic history research has shown, markets and sectors were sometimes also politically controlled and thus, for example, it was not feasible to participate in tobacco exports in Nyasaland when maize prices were low.

Investment is often considered to entail only growth in the modern sector. Thus, assuming that capital formation grew at roughly the same rate as capital goods imports seems reasonable. However, this assumption neglects the importance of land improvement and the planting required to create growth in the export of products such as tea, cocoa, and coffee. Here lagged models can be used, assuming that change in exported output "today" is a result of planting "yesterday" (where the date of "yesterday" will depend on the crops; Szereszewski, 1965: 138–139).[14] This leaves perhaps the biggest stock item still unaccounted for: Roads and dwellings. Estimates for these important items is complicated by the fact the 1953 Standard of National Accounts did give guidance about how to account for them (Seers, 1976). They were introduced in the 1968 national accounts, but countries still measure them in different ways. Per capita allowances, observed outcomes in roads and railroads, and imports of cement, iron, and wood may be feasible proxies.

Instead of introducing any more data, I will attempt to make a few preliminary GDP estimates using the data I have already presented. In what follows, I present the steps I took and the calculations I made to arrive at my new estimates.

The easiest way to start is to make a level estimate for 1931. Population estimates from 1931 from Kuczynski (1937) and Frankema and van Waijenburg (2011) provide data for the per capita local price of subsistence. Multiplying the two (population times consumption basket) provides a lower-end estimate for consumption. Robert Allen (2009) and Frankema and van Waijenburg (2011) both assume that each household consumes three baskets' worth of goods, so larger family size will bias this estimate upward. On the other hand, recall that these are bare-bone subsistence baskets and that anthropometric evidence from the same period indicate that living standards were higher and were increasing (Moradi, 2009). We have no good level data for capital formation, and in the absence of any better estimate, it is simply assumed that investment equals 25 percent of export value. This is higher than the share of exports that were financing capital goods imports, but Szereszewski (1965) used the average ratio of capital formation and exports in his level estimates for the Gold Coast 1891, 1901, and 1911. One would be better off trying to get a sense of the share of savings in household budgets, calculating the share of investment in government expenditures, and, similar to Szereszewski's method, gauging the investment required to support the observed export growth, but I have done this for these figures reported here. The other three items: Government expenditures, exports, and imports, are straightforward and readily available and are displayed in tables 3.18–3.22.

The prices of the subsistence baskets for Uganda, Tanganyika, and Nyasaland are comparatively high. This may mean that prices in the

Table 3.18 *Total exports for Gambia, Gold Coast, Nigeria, Kenya,*
Tanganyika, Uganda, and Nyasaland, selected years, 1896–1965 (in
thousands of 1913 British pounds)

	Gambia	Gold Coast	Nigeria	Kenya	Tanganyika	Uganda	Nyasaland
1895	—	1,104.2	—	—	—	—	—
1903	—	1,131.4	2,718.6	—	304.5	61.0	55.9
1914	914.2	4,879.2	6,072.1	991.9	2,863.8	563.7	180.1
1930	614.6	6,935.4	10,341.5	3,024.6	2,594.8	1,441.9	464.3
1950	573.9	20,266.4	23,508.8	2,734.1	6,169.2	3,041.4	1,884.1
1965	—	17,415.1	49,251.8	5,699.2	13,701.8	—	2,533.1

Source: Colonial reports and blue books (various years).

Table 3.19 *GDP estimates for Gold Coast, Kenya, Tanganyika, Uganda,*
and Nyasaland, 1930 British pounds

	Gold Coast	Kenya	Tanganyika	Uganda	Nyasaland
Consumption	5,573,042	6,681,199	10,700,956	12,321,879	3,926,263
Government expenditures	3,744,010	2,444,793	1,835,000	1,412,241	428,901
Investment	2,477,672	1,080,534	927,000	515,113	165,857
Exports	9,910,688	4,322,136	3,708,000	2,060,453	663,426
Imports	7,562,306	6,831,882	3,142,736	1,363,314	645,636
GDP	14,143,106	7,696,780	14,028,220	14,946,372	4,538,810

Source: Colonial reports and blue books (various years).

Table 3.20 *1930 share in GDP estimates, Gold Coast, Kenya,*
Tanganyika, Uganda, and Nyasaland

	Gold Coast	Kenya	Tanganyika	Uganda	Nyasaland
Consumption	0.39	0.87	0.76	0.82	0.87
Government expenditures	0.26	0.32	0.13	0.09	0.09
Investment	0.18	0.14	0.07	0.03	0.04
Exports	0.70	0.56	0.26	0.14	0.15
Imports	0.53	0.89	0.22	0.09	0.14

Source: Colonial reports and blue books (various years) and my own calculations.

Table 3.21 *GDP per capita estimates, Gold Coast, Kenya, Tanganyika, Uganda, and Nyasaland, 1930*

	Gold Coast	Kenya	Tanganyika	Uganda	Nyasaland
Consumption	1.9	2.2	2.1	3.5	2.4
Government expenditures	1.3	0.8	0.4	0.4	0.3
Investment	0.8	0.4	0.2	0.1	0.1
Exports	3.4	1.4	0.7	0.6	0.4
Imports	2.6	2.2	0.6	0.4	0.4
GDP	4.8	2.5	2.8	4.2	2.8

Source: Colonial reports and blue books (various years).

Table 3.22 *GDP per capita estimates, Gold Coast, Kenya, Tanganyika, Uganda, and Nyasaland, 1950 and 1965*

	Gold Coast	Kenya	Tanganyika	Uganda	Nyasaland
1950	1,122	651	424	687	324
1965	1,393	743	497	779	397

Source: Maddison 2009.

basket are not representative of the prices (or the opportunity cost of the prices) people paid for subsistence in these economies. Thus, it is possible that the total value of consumption is overestimated, in which case GDP is too. In the absence of better data for subsistence, this cannot be readily improved upon. Note, however, that the percentage share of consumption in GDP is consistent with other estimates for other economies. Okigbo (1962) found that it varied from 86 to 88 percent for Nigeria for the period 1950 to 1957. In contrast, Szereszewski found traditional consumption to be 82, 74, and 57 percent of GDP in 1891, 1901, and 1911, respectively. Thus, bearing in mind the rapid economic growth in the Gold Coast after World War I, a reduction toward 39 percent does not seem completely out of bounds. In these very open economies, GDP is very likely to be highly volatile and thus we may get different ratios for different years. Nevertheless, the Maddison estimates (in 1990 Geary-Khamis dollars) seem to bring further support to these 1930 levels.

African Economic Growth, 1900–1950: A New Time Series for British Colonial Africa Based on Historical National Accounts

My review of the data sources seems to indicate that we can meaningfully use historical data to measure economic growth. GDP can be calculated using the expenditure, income, and output approaches. Each approach has different demands in terms of data. The data recorded in the blue books are most relevant to the output approach, which is calculated as the sum of value added by agriculture (A), industry (I) and services (S):

$$GDP = A + I + S$$

The output approach has been used extensively to construct historical national accounts. Simplified versions based only on an agricultural and nonagricultural sector have been applied to the cases of Italy in the period 1270 to 1850 (Malanima, 2011) and Spain from 1300 to 1913 (Álvarez-Nogal and Prados de la Escosura, 2013). More complex versions that expand the nonagricultural sector into industry and services are also common, such as Broadberry et al. (2018) for China from 980 to 1840, Broadberry et al. (2015) for England and Great Britain from 1270 to 1870, Fourie and van Zanden (2013) for the Dutch Cape Colony for 1701 to 1795, Schön and Krantz (2012) for Sweden from 1560 to 1800, and van Zanden and van Leeuwen (2012) for Holland from 1347 to 1807.

Wages, Prices, and Population

The output approach requires information on wages, prices, and population. Using the blue books, I compiled an index of a representative wage in agriculture, industry, and services. It is weighted according to each sector's share of total employment, which is derived from the censuses discussed in the appendix for this chapter.[15] Wages were recorded on an annual, monthly, weekly, or daily basis. In each case, I annualized the wage by assuming 312 working days or 52 working weeks per year, following Frankema and van Waijenburg (2012). When a minimum and maximum wage was documented, I used the average. The new index builds on the work of Frankema and van

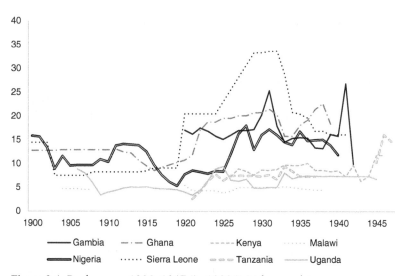

Figure 3.1 Real wages, 1900–1947 (in 1933 British pounds)
Source: Frankema and van Waijenburg (2012).

Waijenburg (2012), who constructed separate series for rural unskilled, urban unskilled, and urban skilled males by aggregating these individual wage rates to yield one representative index. This index series is plotted in Figure 3.1.

The next step is to construct indices of agricultural, nonagricultural, and consumer prices, using data on the median price change from the basket of retail prices that Frankema and van Waijenburg (2012) recorded based on information in the blue books. The agricultural price index is based on the agricultural goods in the consumption basket, such as maize, rice, and wheat. The nonagricultural price index is based on the nonagricultural goods in the consumption basket, such as coal, kerosene, and soap. The classification of agricultural and nonagricultural goods is shown in Appendix Table 3.25. The consumer price index is based on all of the goods listed in that table.

The median consumer price index is preferable to a standard index weighted by consumption. The Federal Reserve Bank of Cleveland produces a median consumer price index, arguing that it provides a clearer signal of inflation. In historical contexts, the problem is likely to be amplified, as the consumption baskets, where they are available, are likely to be based on a small sample of households and

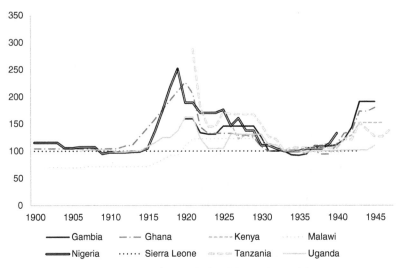

Figure 3.2 Consumer price indices, 1900–1948 (1933 = 100)
Source: Frankema and van Waijenburg (2012).

for a single snapshot in time. Economic historians have also embraced median consumer price indices, as Andersson and Lennard (2019) did in the case of Ireland in the nineteenth and early twentieth centuries. The new consumer price indices for the Gambia, Ghana, Kenya, Malawi, Nigeria, Sierra Leone, Tanzania, and Uganda are shown in Figure 3.2.

Agriculture

Agriculture was the largest sector in the colonial period. Unfortunately, it is not possible to calculate agricultural output using the blue books directly. However, a common approach in output-based historical national accounts is to estimate agricultural production using a consumption function for agricultural goods (Álvarez-Nogal and Prados de la Escosura, 2013; Malanima, 2011; Schön and Krantz, 2012), which is sometimes adjusted for net trade in food to yield agricultural production. Following Allen (1999), the following formula is used, where Q is the volume of agricultural consumption, P is the real price of agricultural goods, I is real income per head, M is the real price of nonagricultural goods, and N is the population. a is a constant and e, g, and b are own-price, income, and cross-price elasticities:

$$Q = a\,P^e\,I^g\,Mb\,N$$

In this equation, P, I, and M have all been deflated by the consumer price index. Following Allen (2000), a is set as 1, e as -0.6, g as 0.5, and b as 0.1. This assumes that agricultural consumption is a positive function of income and the relative price of nonagricultural goods, and is a negative function of the relative price of agricultural goods.

In a closed economy, agricultural consumption is equal to agricultural production, but in an open economy trade should be taken into account. In most studies, scholars assume for simplicity that economies are closed (e.g., Álvarez-Nogal and Prados de la Escosura, 2013; Broadberry et al., 2015; Malanima, 2011) or they multiply Q by the ratio of agricultural production to consumption that is either constant or changes infrequently (Allen, 2000).

In this new data series, I added the net exports of agricultural goods to the series of agricultural consumption to yield agricultural production. This captures the fact that producing cash crops for the export market was an important part of African economic activity. The blue books recorded the import and export of agricultural goods under class 1 ("food, drink and tobacco") and class 2 ("raw materials and articles mainly unmanufactured"). I transcribed the aggregate values of these classes and deflated them by the agricultural price index. Figure 3.3 shows the new series of agricultural output data.

Industry

Industry in pre-independence Africa was the least important sector in terms of its share of output. It consisted of three main branches: building, mining, and manufacturing. I have assumed that building grew in line with population, as did Broadberry et al. (2015) and Broadberry et al. (2018), Fourie and van Zanden (2013), and Schön and Krantz (2012). The blue books recorded both the value and the volume of mining. They did not record manufacturing output; a typical blue book for a colony in Africa notes that "no important manufactories exist and no information is available regarding native industries." Following Broadberry et al. (2018), I used population as a proxy for manufacturing. The new indices of industrial output are shown in Figure 3.4.

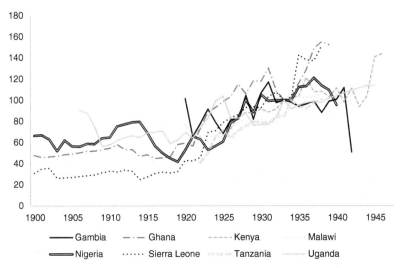

Figure 3.3 Agricultural output, 1900–1946 (1933 = 100)
Source: Author's calculations drawing on blue book data and Allen (1999).

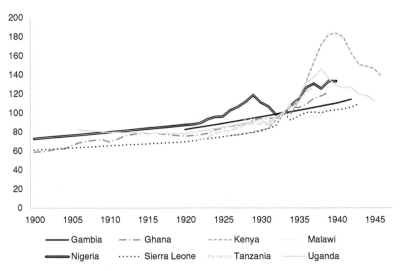

Figure 3.4 Industrial output, 1900–1946 (1933 = 100)
Source: Author's calculations drawing on blue book data and Broadberry et al.
(2015).

Services

Services were a relatively important sector of the African economy before independence. They included communications, distribution, domestic services, finance, government, housing, and transport. Communications is the revenue from the "posts and telegraphs," which included revenue from telegraph and telephone receipts, postage for letters and parcels, and income from wireless licenses, among other things, deflated by the services deflator. Distribution is a weighted average of exports (60 percent) and industrial output (40 percent), as in Broadberry et al. (2015). I deflated exports using a weighted average of the agricultural and industrial price indices, deriving the weights from the data in Table 3.23. I used population as a proxy for domestic services and housing, following Broadberry et al. (2015). Finance is based on the number of banks in operation (Broadberry et al., 2015). Government is measured as total government revenue (Broadberry et al., 2015) deflated by the services deflator. Transport is the revenue from railways and tramways deflated by the services deflator. I assumed that other services grew in line with the weighted average of these services. Figure 3.5 shows the new series of output from services.

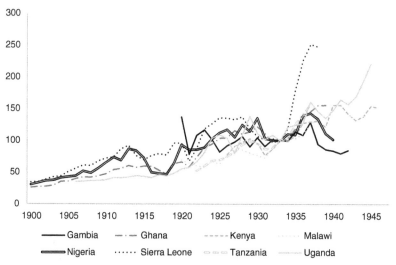

Figure 3.5 Service sector output, 1900–1946 (1933 = 100)
Source: Author's calculations drawing on blue book data and Broadberry et al. (2015).

Gross Domestic Product

In order to aggregate the branch indices into sectoral indices, a benchmark is needed that relates each branch to a sector. I used Okigbo's (1962) estimate of nominal GDP for Nigeria in 1950 for the weights for the branches and sectors as reported in Table 3.23.

The indices of the volume of production from agriculture, industry, and services can be converted into nominal indices by multiplying the respective volume index by a respective price index. For agriculture, the deflator is the agricultural price index described above. For industry, the deflator is a weighted average of the price indices for building, mining, and manufacturing.[16] The index of nominal industrial wages described above serves as the proxy for building prices, as in Broadberry et al. (2015). I calculated mining prices using the aforementioned values and volumes of mining output. The nonagricultural price index discussed above serves as the proxy for manufacturing prices. The weights are based on the industrial output shares in Table 3.23. For services, the deflator is a weighted average of distribution prices and other prices for services. Distribution prices are a weighted average

Table 3.23 *Sectoral share of nominal GDP, 1933 (percent)*

Sector	Share
Agriculture	65.9
Industry	6.4
Building	1.6
Mining	1.1
Manufacturing	3.7
Services	27.7
Communications	0.4
Distribution	10.6
Domestic services	0.5
Finance	0.1
Government	2.1
Housing	1.2
Transport	4.5
Other services	8.4
Total	100.0

Source: Derived from Okigbo (1962).

of agricultural and industrial prices, as in Broadberry et al. (2015). Other prices for services are the index of nominal services wages described above, as in Álvarez-Nogal and Prados de la Escosura (2013) and Broadberry et al. (2015); the weights are calculated from the data in Table 3.23.

The indices for real GDP are a weighted average of the sectoral indices. The GDP deflators are a weighted average of the sectoral deflators. The weights are listed in Table 3.2. The indices of nominal GDP are calculated by multiplying real GDP and the GDP deflator.

An important consideration is whether the shares, which were derived from Nigerian national accounts, are appropriate for the other economies studied here. Evidence from the censuses indicates that the occupational structure was similar across all of the economies. I take that information to support the assumption that labor productivity in each sector was equivalent across economies.

To convert the indices into the level of GDP, I multiplied the benchmark GDP level estimates reported in Table 3.23 from Prados de la Escosura (2012) by population data from Frankema and Jerven (2014), where 1933 = 100. For the first half of the twentieth century, Prados de la Escosura (2012) reported benchmarks for 1900, 1913, 1925, 1929, 1933, 1938, and 1950. The only benchmarks for which there are GDP estimates for all countries are 1929 and 1933. As the value-added shares in Table 3.24 are based on Nigeria in 1950, I chose 1933 because it is closer to 1950.

Table 3.24 *GDP per capita, selected African countries, 1933 (in 1990 international dollars)*

Country	GDP
Gambia	486
Ghana	740
Kenya	503
Malawi	300
Nigeria	595
Sierra Leone	482
Tanzania	334
Uganda	569

Source: My calculations based on blue book data and Prados de la Escosura (2012).

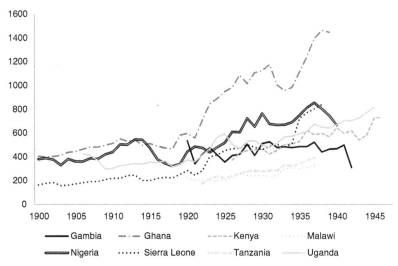

Figure 3.6 African GDP per capita, 1900–1946 (1990 international dollars)
Source: Author's calculations based on blue book data and Prados de la Escosura (2012).

The results confirm expectations and are consistent with the patterns in real wages and trade discussed in previous sections. While I have made these GDP estimates with sparse historical data and the data regarding the agricultural sector and food consumption in particular rest on heavy assumptions, there is some comfort in the level of corroborating evidence and the fact that I reached similar findings using different sets of assumptions and methods. These growth estimates rest in part on a sector benchmark from the 1950s, but it is reassuring to have found a similar path of growth using an 1891 benchmark and letting food consumption be proportional to population growth (Jerven, 2014b). This new GDP series on British colonial Africa together with the other evidence put forward by other scholars discussed here allows for a changed interpretation of economic growth in the twentieth century.

New Perspectives on African Economic Growth in the Twentieth Century

What emerges is quite a different image of Africa and economic growth on the continent in the twentieth century. While the past century has been widely summarized as a "growth tragedy" (Easterly and Levine, 1997; Artadi and Sala-i-Martín, 2003), the new data series described here shows rapid and widespread economic growth from the late 1890s that was sustained into the 1970s. Growth was only temporarily interrupted in the 1980s, and the continent has returned to growth since the mid-1990s. This changes the narrative from the hopeless continent to the hopeful continent (Jerven, 2015). The depth of the crisis in the 1980s wiped away some of the economic gains made in the long period of growth leading up to it, but the scholarly conclusion that economic growth in Africa was something that was chronically failed does not hold up to the historical evidence.

In the next chapter, I will review the evidence on taxation in the twentieth century and demonstrate that the pattern in the new GDP estimates hold up in the revenue data: Growth from the late 1800s and into the 1970s, a decline in the 1980s, and a return to growth in the 1990s. Chapter 4 is supported by a continent-wide dataset. Although it shows a great deal of variation among countries, the pattern throughout the continent is robust. The GDP growth evidence reviewed here has drawn upon a nonrandom sample of most of the British colonies from the early 1900s to the late 1940s. The question of whether that pattern of growth was present in the French, Belgian, German, and Portuguese colonies is testable. Similar data availability means that the same methods of historical national accounting could be used for these countries.

4 State Capacity across the Twentieth Century: Evidence from Taxation

WITH THILO ALBERS AND MARVIN SUESSE[*]

There is no question that taxes matter for economic development and state formation. Not only is there an obvious link between the capacity of a state to collect taxes and its ability to deliver development outcomes, such as expenditures and investments. More subtly, there is indirect evidence that taxation stimulates economic and political development to some degree because it strengthens the contract between citizens and the state (Besley and Persson, 2014). A long-standing (although sometimes disappointingly vague) conversation in development economics and development studies has looked at how governance and institutions matter (Jerven, 2015). Studying the institutions that tax, and measuring how much they collect, seems like an obvious way of pinning down a question of potentially great importance.

How have African states evolved over time? Thilo Albers, Marvin Suesse, and I have studied this question by compiling data on the composition of government revenue and the level of taxation for all territories in Africa from 1900 to 2010 (Albers et al., 2020). This dataset is the result of a first attempt to establish a consistent, long time series on government revenue for the entire continent, thus opening up new lines of inquiry into the evolution of African statehood. The data allow for a close examination of the link between the capacity of African states to collect taxes and their ability to deliver development outcomes, such as expenditures and investments. Studying the fiscal institutions of African states also provides an easily observable and measurable way of tracing the evolution of institutions through the colonial and postcolonial era.

This chapter makes a contribution toward analyzing levels and trends in taxation with reasonable accuracy over time and space for African countries by proposing a new dataset for African countries

---

[*] Thilo Albers is a postdoctoral researcher at Humboldt University Berlin. Marvin Suesse is Assistant Professor in Economics at Trinity College Dublin.

across the twentieth century. The main metric that we emphasize in this chapter is the analysis of a general continent-wide trend in taxation. Of course, there is much variation among African states, which we analyze elsewhere (Albers et al., 2020). Nonetheless, the focus on a single trend is warranted by an influential literature in the social sciences stressing the genesis and evolution of a particular type of "African state," with its supposedly distinct pathology (Herbst, 2000). This hypothesized pathology is often thought to be evident in an inability by the "African state" to enforce rules within its jurisdiction or to collect taxes. The purpose of this chapter is not to argue that such a specific "African state" exists. Rather, we demonstrate that, even if we accept the premise of a singular type of "African state," this state has been marked by a remarkable and dynamic *growth* in tax collection. In other words, the core argument concerning the pathology of weak African statehood does not correspond to empirical reality, even if considered on its own terms, and should therefore be called into question. In fact, our new dataset shows growth in real tax revenues from the beginning of the nineteenth century with a first peak around 1940. After declines or plateaus, we see marked increases through the 1960s and into the 1970s, that is after independence. A not-so-marked second peak in the 1970s is followed by a decline into the 1980s. There was a significant increase in the late decades of the twentieth century through the 2010s.

What Do We Know about Taxation in Sub-Saharan Africa?

The literature on economic development has emphasized that institutions determine economic performance. Douglas North (1990) pioneered this work, although the reasons why these institutions persist is somewhat unclear in his analysis. Work by Daron Acemoğlu, Simon Johnson, and James Robinson (2001) and Nathan Nunn (2008) has emphasized the role of institutions in determining the performance of countries in sub-Saharan Africa. More recently, a growing body of literature has highlighted the impact of historical tax regimes on present fiscal capacity (Mkandawire, 2010), government corruption (Gardner, 2010), and the quality of governance (Baskaran and Bigsten, 2012).

Jonathan Di John (2009) suggests that tax collection is one of the most powerful lenses for looking at the legitimacy of the state. Timothy

Besley and Torsten Persson (2014: 100) call taxation "the core of state development." It plays an essential role in a state's ability to carry out its responsibilities.

However, relatively little attention has been paid to getting the data on taxation right. We know very little about the history of taxation in sub-Saharan Africa because of two different problems. The first is that little systematized data about taxation in the long run in Africa exists. As we show below, the information that is available generally relies on sporadic data points from colonial blue books, or for more recent periods, international datasets or country-specific reports by organizations such as the International Monetary Fund (IMF).

However, we do have indicative evidence. The early colonial period was characterized by skepticism about the economic progress of the African colonies, particularly after the discovery that domestic populations were significantly smaller than had originally been estimated (Green, 2012: 231). This led to a reluctance on the part of both colonial treasuries and private capital to invest in the region and colonies were left to fund as much of their expenditures from domestic sources as possible (Gardner, 2010: 215).

Under these conditions, colonial rulers adopted penny-pinching policies and policies of revenue neutrality to prevent colonies from being a financial drain on the metropoles (Green, 2012: 231). Consequently, colonial administrations were severely understaffed; they have characterized as being "a gimcrack effort run by two men and a dog" (Kirk-Greene, 1980: 26). Complicating the situation further was the fact that the relatively low economic activity of many regions precluded the generation of significant levels of customs revenue (Gardner, 2010: 217), especially given the increasing ability of merchants and settlers to evade taxes levied on them (Green, 2012: 231; Young, 1994: 126).

As a result, revenue generation in many territories soon focused on imposing direct taxes (Frankema and van Waijenburg, 2014: 393). Head or hut taxes and poll taxes were quickly imposed almost everywhere. In addition to being a tool for generating revenue, these taxes helped colonizers pursue broader social goals, particularly the goal of channeling domestic labor into wage labor (Young 1994: 126–127). However, the combination of delegating the task of collecting direct taxes to colonial administrators and limited population data created substantial opportunities to misappropriate tax revenue. Leigh

Gardner (2010) provides a summary of the growth of hut and poll taxes at the beginning of the nineteenth century and suggests that corruption in colonial times could have a long-term effect on state capacities now.

Barbara Bush and Josephine Maltby (2004) describe how taxation was used for the purpose of "civilizing" colonial subjects in West Africa. While this entailed a higher degree of effort to extract tax revenue, direct taxation of the population necessitated the increased monetarization of a society and the creation of a wage labor class. Bush and Maltby's article is mostly qualitative, describing the evolution of tax policy in West Africa and its impact on the creation of a group consciousness and local resistance to such policies. Yet it is helpful in its depiction of the different strategies of taxation colonial administrators used in the region and the different responses domestic populations had available to them. The conclusion we can draw is that a politics of taxation evolved that was heavily influenced by local circumstances.

The broader theoretical and empirical literature in African economic development has paid less attention to taxation *per se*, but its focus on the role of institutions nonetheless informs our approach. The main lessons we take from this literature is that, firstly, institutions matter for economic performance. They do this, secondly, because they are said to persist over long periods of time (decades, sometimes centuries). However, we note that the specific causal factors and the mechanism or channels by which these institutions persist is somewhat unclear in the literature (North, 1990). An influential branch of the literature has sought the origins of comparative development in the identity of the colonizer in a global sample of countries, distinguishing between French and British approaches to colonial rule (La Porta et al., 2008). Works by Acemoğlu et al. (2001), Nunn (2008), and Michalopoulos and Papaioannou (2010) have emphasized that bad institutional arrangements historically imposed upon African polities through colonialism or the slave trade have remained essentially unchanged. Yet we are given little explanation as to the nature of this persistence. The state may be the most important macro-institution to analyze, but what role do essential functions of the state, such as taxation and spending, play in this persistence?

An exception to this lack of focus on taxation from the mainstream literature in economics is the work by Besley and Persson (2014). Although it is not primarily concerned with African states *per se*, this approach emphasizes how low investment in the institutional apparatus required to collect direct taxes can lead to persistently underfunded public services. This can have economic – and political – consequences. As Besley and Persson (2014: 100) note, "The power to tax is about much more than raising tax revenues – it is at the core of state development."

To summarize, the analysis in the literature so far has suggested that the effects of some institutions, in particular colonial political, economic, and social structures, could have persisted from colonial times into the present day. A number of contributions find a relationship between a historical variable that directly captures the shape of institutions or serves as a proxy for them. Many argue that an instrumental variable captures exogenous variation in institutional change of some sort. In turn, these authors show that these variables correlate with present-day outcomes (often GDP per capita today). They then conclude that history has a persistent causal effect on income that is determined by the strength or shape of institutions more generally, and sometimes by the state more specifically.

These works have been subject to a range of criticisms, some noted here already. In particular, it is important to highlight the problem that Gareth Austin (2008) referred to as "the compression of history." Work in this tradition essentially argues that one variable from the past has had a persistent effect on present-day circumstances. Without a database such as the one we provide in the underlying working paper (Albers et al., 2020), these approaches require readers to take a leap of faith and believe that the correlations the authors have found hold true over time. Such claims should at least be substantiated by evidence that institutions, say the particular legal code (French or British) used by colonizers, had an effect on outcomes in 2010 as well as in 1960. A similar point made about institutions in general can be made about tax-collecting institutions in particular: The lack of time-series data on taxation for African countries has meant that the literature has focused on the important but reductive question of why African countries seem to tax so little at present.

Yet despite the importance of taxation, large gaps in our knowledge of rates and trends in collecting tax revenue exist. As we explain below, two problems lay at the origin of this lacuna. The first is that while data on taxation in African countries does exist, it has proven hard to collect because data exist in different locations and are categorized differently from country to country and even within countries from year to year.

The second is that it is difficult to express revenue data in a way that is directly comparable over time and space. Because of these two issues, our understanding of colonial fiscal policy is clouded by a lack of systematic data. The information that does exist has often been collected for the purpose of individual research. While this is a laudable goal at any rate, we require an accessible and centralized dataset to move beyond vague discussions of persistence and "weak" African states. We first turn to discussing the current availability of consistent data on African taxation, which has improved somewhat in recent years, before turning to our own solution to the data problem.

The Data Problem

There has been some informal division of labor in the literature on the economics, economic history, and history of Africa (Manning, 1987). This is important for understanding the shape of the literature and the available datasets. One division relates to time periods. Until 2010, economists typically did work on the postcolonial period and historians worked on the colonial period (Jerven, 2011a). This has had a number of effects. First, historians are less interested in measuring taxation in numbers (compared to econometricians, for whom that is the main purpose of using an archive) and more interested in describing taxation as statecraft, a political process and a meeting between state and citizen. Second, historians working on Africa have tended to write monographs on one country. Historians are typically trained to produce in-depth studies of one location rather than cross-country comparisons. Thus, while the data has been available, they have not been compiled yet.

For the purposes of analyzing the current state of the literature, we follow the conventional periodization of African history into the precolonial, colonial, and postcolonial periods.[1] Each period has its own distinct data problems, and our own work is limited to an investigation of the colonial and postcolonial periods. Although there are many states to study in the long precolonial period, quantitative state records are scarce. Thus, it is likely not possible that someone will be able to create annual comparable time series for a range of states that could offer a clear comparison.[2] The early rise of colonial taxation and the extent to which this replaced or supplemented taxation in the precolonial period remains a subject that requires nuanced historical judgment and cannot be readily settled with time-series data. The precolonial period therefore deserves more attention in future case-study-oriented research (Reid, 2011).

The issue for the colonial and postcolonial periods is quite different. Here the records do exist, but either they have not been compiled or they have been partially compiled but not crafted into in a continent-wide database that allows for systematic comparisons.

Our understanding of colonial taxation is improving as the literature on the developmental legacies of colonial institutions improves. Most of this research has been done on the British and (to a lesser extent) French colonies. A small amount of comparative work has been done across colonial empires. Different languages and the far-flung locations of archives means that creating a harmonized database is resource intensive, and no one has yet tried to compile a continent-wide dataset for the colonial period. Instead of using countries as the unit of analysis, this research has tended to focus on colonizers. This makes perfect sense, in particular for a scholar for whom the language and location of the archives matters a great deal. Thus, we have authors who have collected and analyzed data for the Portuguese empire in Africa (Alexopoulou, 2018; Havik, 2012) and for the French empire in Africa (Andersson, 2018) and beyond (Cogneau et al., 2018). Similarly, for the British Empire there are papers on British Africa (Frankema, 2011) and the British empire as a whole (Frankema, 2010). Language limitations may explain why there is no continent-wide dataset yet, and even if data are produced on one part of the region or one country, it is not always published in a shareable fashion.

Table 4.1 reports some of the main pieces of work on the topic of colonial taxation that have appeared in the past decade.[3] More comparable data points have become available, and there are now some comparative publications (Frankema and van Waijenburg, 2014).

This literature confirms that, in most areas, the colonial period was characterized by a marked increase in direct taxation.[4] These include the hut or head taxes and poll taxes of the time, which assigned flat taxes across individuals or households. As stated, many explanations have been used to explain this trend, including the low administrative capacity of the colonies and the desire to incorporate indigenous populations into wage work. Our information about taxation is far less abundant starting with the end of World War II. That period was particularly tumultuous for the region. Decolonization and influxes

Table 4.1 *Coverage of colonial taxation in Africa in the economic and developmental economic literature, 2010–2020*

Countries/Area	Time period	Authors
Francophone West Africa Benin, Côte d'Ivoire, Niger and Senegal	1850–2010	Andersson (2018)
The French Empire Covers almost the entire second French colonial empire. Except for the Indochinese Union, most colonies were in Africa: Algeria, Tunisia and Morocco, the federations of French West Africa and French Equatorial Africa, Togo, Cameroon, and Madagascar.*	1830–1962	Cogneau et al. (2018)
Portuguese Africa Mozambique and Angola	1850s–1970s	Alexopoulou (2018)
Portuguese Africa Mozambique, Angola, and Guinea	Late 1800s– 1950s	Havik (2015)
British Africa Gambia, Sierra Leone, Gold Coast, Nigeria, Nyasaland, Kenya, Uganda, and Mauritius (some data on New Zealand is included)	1880–1940	Frankema (2011)
British Africa/Empire East and Southern Africa: Bechuanaland, Northern Rhodesia, Nyasaland Protectorate, Kenya, and Tanganyika Territory West Africa: Gambia, Sierra Leone, Gold Coast, Nigeria, Mauritius (and India) Also includes some data on the United Kingdom and the Dominions: Australia, New Zealand, Canada, and Union of South Africa.	1870–1940	Frankema (2010)
French and British Africa **French West Africa** Ivory Coast, Dahomey, French Guinea, Upper Volta, Mauritania, Niger, Senegal, and French Sudan	ca. 1880–1940	Frankema and van Waijenburg (2014)

Table 4.1 (*cont.*)

Countries/Area	Time period	Authors
French Equatorial Africa		
French Congo, French Gabon, Ubangi-Shari, and Chad		
French Africa other		
Cameroon, Madagascar, Somaliland, Togo, and Réunion		
British West Africa		
Gambia, Gold Coast, Nigeria, and Sierra Leone		
British East Africa (BEA)		
Bechuanaland, Kenya, Northern Rhodesia, Nyasaland, Uganda, and Tanganyika		
British Africa other		
Mauritius		

Note: A comparable table appears in the online data appendix of Albers et al. (2020). The majority of data are from the early twentieth century; 1911, 1920, 1925, 1929, 1934, and 1937 are key years.

* Dataset corresponds to twenty-one present-day countries: Algeria, Morocco, and Tunisia in North Africa; Benin, Burkina Faso, Cameroon, Chad, Central African Republic, Congo-Brazzaville, Cote d'Ivoire, Gabon, Guinea, Madagascar, Mali, Mauritania, Niger, Senegal, and Togo in sub-Saharan Africa; and Vietnam, Laos, and Cambodia in Southeast Asia.

of aid and loans that began in the 1950s may have had a lasting effect on fiscal capacity in sub-Saharan Africa.

However, even if the raw data are available at least in piecemeal fashion, the key problem of comparability remains. Comparability is only attained if tax revenues can be expressed in standardized categories, in real per capita terms. The comparability problem, therefore, stems from three sources. For one, the categorization of revenues into distinct categories, for example direct or indirect taxes, differs substantially between reporting countries. It differed substantially even within colonial empires, and was changed frequently over time by rulers, both colonial and independent. The absence of standardized reporting across colonial empires and legal traditions compounds this issue. Secondly, noncomprehensive censuses of population hinder the investigation of per capita tax burdens – an issue that has been discussed elsewhere in this volume. Thirdly, it is not meaningful to compare nominal revenue figures over time, in the presence of the high bouts of inflation experienced by many African states, especially in the late 1970s and 1980s. The standard solution to this problem has been to express taxation as a share of GDP. Yet as discussed already, such a ratio is either impossible to calculate or misleading in the absence of reliable GDP figures.

One of the most important efforts to alleviate the comparability constraint has been made by Ewout Frankema (2011), who investigates revenue and expenditures in British Africa from 1880 to 1940. In his evaluation of the divergence of fiscal policies in British West Africa and East Africa, he calculated gross public revenue and tax burdens for eight colonies using information from colonial blue books and other archival sources. Frankema calculated a tax burden measure based on fiscal revenue per capita divided by the daily wage of an adult male worker (Frankema, 2011: 139). This equates to the average number of male workdays required to meet the tax burden imposed on the population in eight British colonies.

Building on this data, Frankema and van Waijenburg (2012) compared fiscal policies in British and French colonial Africa from 1880 to 1940, using data from a variety of colonial records (Table 4.2). They emphasize that local conditions tended to override metropolitan blueprints for colonial governance. The sample of countries they covered is larger than the ones Frankema (2011) studied and is subdivided by the nationality of the colonizer, the region of Africa, and other geographical considerations.

A significant finding of this article is that in colonial Africa, gross revenue per capita was negatively correlated with the proportion of direct taxes levied on the population. The authors conclude that when

Table 4.2 *Number of countries covered in Frankema and van Waijenburg (2012)*

	East Africa	West Africa	Other
Britain	6	4	1
France	4	8	5

the state was able to raise sufficient capital through other means (taxing trade, for example), governments imposed relatively low direct taxes (Frankema and van Waijenburg, 2012). One shortcoming of this research is that it details only a select number of years from the period 1880 to 1940 (namely, 1911, 1920, 1925, 1929, 1934, and 1937), providing snapshots in time from which to infer trends rather than consistent and transparent time-series data.

While colonial tax policy is traditionally thought to have been shaped by the nationality of the colonizer, the literature has highlighted the importance of local conditions over central policies. Frankema and van Waijenburg (2012) contribute to this by comparing official tax rates in urban centers to those of the poorest rural region in African countries. They note that these discrepancies were more pronounced in French colonies and that the French adjusted their tax rates more frequently. This was part of a broader trend among colonizers of flexible taxation depending on local circumstances, such as perceived indigenous hostility and ability to pay.

Postcolonial Period

There is some disruption in the datasets in the late colonial period and the World War II years, but after 1960 many countries published official statistics in a semi-regular fashion in their own statistical abstracts and in reporting to UN agencies and other international organizations. However, the impact of financial difficulties on statistical reporting in most African economies in the late 1970s to the early 1990s has been well noted. The term "lost decades" has been used to refer to the 1980s and the 1990s not only in terms of economic growth, but also in terms of statistical record keeping (Jerven, 2013).

The availability of African data on taxation has improved since 1990. The emergence of international datasets, the increased emphasis (including on the part of donors) on fiscal capacity, and the recognition of the importance of statistics have all highlighted the need for time-series data that help illuminate trends. Unfortunately, missing or inconsistent observations and inconsistencies in data collection methods have necessitated subjective decisions about which observations to include and how to deal with missing information. Some of the techniques for responding to these problems leave room for improvement,

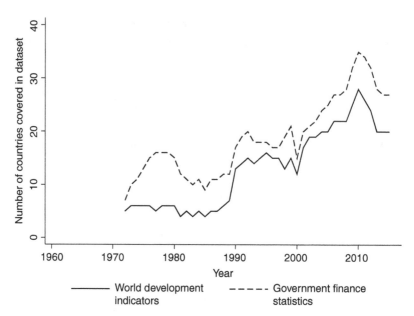

Figure 4.1 Countries covered by international databases of international organizations (September 2018)
This figure shows the coverage for revenue data of the two datasets by year. It is also printed in the online data appendix of Albers et al., (2020).

and there is still room to increase the reliability of the data. We now turn to analyzing these data sources.

The International Monetary Fund's Government Finance Statistics (GFS) is a dataset of revenue and expenditure statistics from countries around the world. It provides four main tax measures: Total taxes, trade taxes, direct taxes, and indirect taxes along with data on grants and other types of revenue. Even if we focus on the total revenue data and include North African countries as in Figure 4.1, the gaps are considerable. The coverage is bad in the 1970s, worse in the 1980s, and does not even cover half of the African countries in the 1990s. After stagnation throughout that decade, reporting improved in the 2000s. However, the graph highlights another major concern as we are getting closer to the present: The time lag in publication is substantial. As of 2018 the peak of the reporting countries was still in 2010, amounting to 35 countries. Figure 4.1 also compares the IMF GFS data to another major international resource for research and policy-making – the

World Development Indicators. The problems described above apply to both of these databases and even more so to the World Development Indicators.

The publication lags for African countries and the sparse coverage of the recent past are concerning. Potentially more problematic still is the fact that the data that is available has been criticized for its lack of consistency across individual countries. That is because the IMF generally publishes data that national statistical offices report to it. However, these national offices may not be (and often are not) consistent in how they track revenue and expenditure data. Thus, the data from the national statistical offices made available via the IMF Government Finance Statistics has rightly been criticized for both its lack of coverage and its inconsistent reliability (Jerven, 2016a).

Faced with basic data availability issues, researchers have made ad hoc patches to the IMF database. One example of this is Thushyanthan Baskaran and Arne Bigsten's (2012) analysis of the relationship between fiscal capacity and governance quality in sub-Saharan Africa. They constructed a dataset of thirty-one sub-Saharan African countries for the period 1990–2005. To do this, they combined data from the OECD's African Economic Outlook dataset with the World Bank's Africa Development Indicators. Motivated by a high correlation (0.9) between these two datasets, the authors used the one dataset to fill in missing data in the other. A similar strategy of merging existing datasets has been used by Wilson Prichard and David Leonard (2010: 658). This resulted in a new dataset of tax statistics for sub-Saharan Africa, covering forty-five countries from 1972 to 2005. Approximately 7–20 percent of observations remain missing, depending on the criteria employed. A footnote states that "a detailed description of the process for assembling and cleaning the data is beyond the scope of this paper. Additional information and the cleaned data are available directly from the authors" (671).

Building on earlier work, Mario Mansour increased the coverage of data on taxation to 1980–2010 for a sample of forty-one countries in sub-Saharan Africa (Keen and Mansour, 2010; Mansour, 2014). Taking the GFS as a starting point, Mansour augments and validates the information with data from IMF staff reports and statistical appendices created by various Article IV surveillance and program missions. His dataset improves on the main aggregates in the GFS (total, trade, direct, and indirect taxes) with seven different constituent series (the original four plus corporate, individual, and resource taxes). The coverage across these series is commendable because relatively few gaps exist in the data (352 of 8,897 observations are missing, the majority in the corporate and individual tax series). Wilson Prichard (2016: 58) viewed this as one of the stronger ad hoc datasets but argued that its narrow scope (in terms of both regional coverage and revenue variables) limits its applicability to research.

While these ad hoc datasets were efforts to substitute for or improve upon the GFS, they led to a new set of problems. They have collectively been criticized for both a lack of transparency and a lack of accessibility for the purpose of reproducing data/results. The problem is that some of the data problems were solved by drawing upon internal data sources at the IMF and it is unclear when a data point is the estimate of an IMF staff member and when it is an actual official estimate. Inconsistencies in data collection and data shaping makes comparability across datasets difficult if not impossible. It is telling that researchers using the same research design have come to different conclusions depending on which dataset they used (Prichard et al., 2016: 13–15).

Prichard's work in filling the gaps in the contemporary database was continued in a project housed at the International Centre for Tax and Development that ultimately led to the publication of the Government Revenue Dataset (Prichard, 2016). While Prichard admits that the series is still plagued by methodological problems, it is valuable because of his efforts to provide consistent and comparable data for African economies. The dataset covers forty of forty-two sub-Saharan Africa countries for the period 1990–2009. It has recently been extended back to the 1980s and is now hosted by UNU-WIDER. Although one may argue that the timespan covered is still brief by historical standards, a large benefit of the dataset is its comprehensive coverage of the region. Highlighting problems and inconsistencies across sources in both the numerator and denominator of this measure, Prichard and colleagues have provided a detailed explanation of the six steps they took to construct the dataset (Prichard et al. 2016: 17–29):

1. Develop a standard classification scheme that can accommodate data from multiple sources.
2. Survey existing cross-country datasets.
3. Systematically compile data from IMF Article IV reports, using them to fill in gaps in the series.

4. Adopt a common GDP series in order to eliminate discontinuities.
5. Carefully merge data from these sources into a single dataset, with applicable cleaning up after the merge.
6. Develop a composite dataset that draws on central and general government data in order to provide the most accurate possible picture of national revenue collection.

The authors are quick to highlight their own concerns with the data, particularly the fact that some of the data points used are inconsistent with surrounding observations and trends. The authors also caution that they used a degree of subjectivity when needing to decide between different but equally plausible observations.

Looking across all of the sources we have discussed here, one might argue that the reliability of the data is still a source of concern. Merging existing datasets necessitates some level of subjectivity about how to rank each dataset and how to respond to any resulting inconsistencies. At the same time, relying on national statistical offices for primary data collection is problematic because a country's statistical capacity can have a significant impact on the accuracy and reliability of the statistics it produces (Jerven, 2013). If this source of data is not evaluated carefully, researchers can miss or overlook inconsistencies and introduce bias into their analysis. This problem is exacerbated by the fact that the poorest countries tend to have the lowest statistical capacities.

In sum, the pre-1960 information that is available generally relies on data from colonial archives that have not been harmonized across the African continent. There are large gaps in comprehensive data from the 1940s to the 1980s. For those decades, data are available in statistical abstracts, country reports, and monographic research but not in comprehensive cross-country datasets. More recently, country-focused reporting has given way to international datasets such as that provided by the International Monetary Fund, yet these databases also have gaps, and researchers have sometimes filled those gaps from unofficial sources.

Overall, we still do not have a reliable way of connecting colonial fiscal statistics to present-day statistics because of the lack of available data for the middle of the twentieth century. When these gaps in information are filled, we will be better able to connect colonial fiscal institutions with their possibly enduring postcolonial legacies. The central contribution of this chapter is to present a new dataset and the methods used to create it. This will allow for a better evaluation of arguments surrounding the "weakness" of African states, and the themes of persistence and development by researchers.

Tackling the Data Problem

Does Nigeria tax more today than it did ten years ago? Thirty years ago? Five decades ago? A century ago? The data problem is such that we do not readily have answers to these questions. As explained, no single dataset exists. We therefore set out to fill this gap in our understanding of Africa's political economy. As we have argued, this gap is there for a reason – there is a genuine data problem. It makes sense to approach data problems across three dimensions: availability, reliability, and validity.

Availability refers simply to the question whether some data are available or not. The existing online databases, the ICTD/UNU-WIDER dataset providing the best coverage among them, only go back to the 1980s. Most research on the pre-independence period has remained focused on either building a consistent time series for a few polities or taking snapshots for a cross-section of countries. There are generally large gaps between 1950s and 1980, a period so critical in the development of African statehood. These gaps in availability often hinder if not prevent a systematic analysis of the dynamic developments in the political economy of many African polities over the past century. We know that such data gaps are non-random, historically and for the more recent past. This is particularly obvious for the more recent data: Data are missing in times of economic or political change (e.g., decolonization, economic liberalization under IMF auspices) or for those countries where "development" in a conventional sense has failed. Econometrically, working with missing data that is correlated with the variables under study presents huge challenges that limit the wider applicability of existing datasets.

To overcome the availability problem, we follow the approach of many contributions to the renaissance African economic history is experiencing (Austin and Broadberry, 2014; Jerven et al., 2012). Much of the work that is being done is exactly this kind of painstaking work of unearthing and harmonizing unused historical sources. In doing so we build on the previously described work, which mainly aims to carry out comparisons across a few key years in colonial empires (e.g., Frankema, 2010, 2011), or focuses on case studies (e.g., Gardner, 2012). The key difference from those studies is our geographical and temporal coverage. By drawing fully upon the data available from 1900 to the 2010s across almost all African continental polities, we hope to place the research community in a much better position to answer questions regarding structural change, development, and persistence over the long run.

The second dimension of the data problem is reliability. Reliability relates to whether measures are reliable over time and space so that data errors do not bias the data series. In principle, it seems simple enough, for instance, to compare the 2010 tax receipts in one country with the 1920 tax receipts. However, there may have been changes in legal definitions of tax and substantive changes in how taxes and duties are levied and recorded so that categories of indirect and direct taxation may not be directly comparable over time. To understand the practical importance of this problem, consider business taxation today and 100 years ago. Historically, direct business taxation was carried out by requiring the owner to buy a license, whereas today the businesses are often required to pay income tax. For the limited role of personal income tax, see Bird and Zolt (2005). Yet, in historical summaries licenses are often paired with fees, the latter of which is clearly not a form of direct taxation. Disaggregation and reclassification for an intertemporal comparison thus become absolutely necessary. In sum, analyzing tax data over time requires the reliability of the comparison. We aim to ensure the reliability by retroactively applying modern accounting standards to historical data.

The final dimension of the data problem is the validity of the measure itself. Having made the data comparable in its definitions, we are interested in moving beyond its nominal value. We thus require a valid deflator, that is a variable that allows us to convert the nominal tax data into real values. In many modern studies, taxes are typically expressed as a share of GDP. We know that calculating GDP levels is not an exact science. The most famous recent examples include the 89 percent increases in GDP in Nigeria (Jerven, 2015). Smaller adjustments that are in the order of 20 to 30 percent would still cause noise in any series, invalidating a comparison of tax as a share of GDP in a country over time or across countries. While it is possible to smooth out the effects and/or correct for changes in definitions across time, comparisons across space for more than a few counties will invariably involve a rather big leap of faith for data users. The questions of validity and reliability of the basic numbers are therefore existential to the validity of any comparative approach.

In our joint work, we have sought to minimize these leaps of faith as much as possible by providing a consistent time series of revenue collection. Our primary contribution is to improve data availability and quality, but we also make a contribution by expressing the tax data and its components in real terms. We do this through expressing all magnitudes in constant terms, which is achieved by deflating it with urban wages and dividing it by the population. The details of this strategy are described below.

Data Strategy

Previous researchers who have compiled fiscal datasets have focused on time periods before independence (see, e.g., Frankema, 2010; Frankema, 2011; and Frankema and van Waijenburg, 2014) or on very recent periods (see, e.g., Ahlerup et al., 2014). The dataset we have constructed so far is part of an effort to produce a first systematic and continuous account of fiscal capacity in Africa from colonial times until today. We are especially grateful to other researchers, especially Ewout Frankema and Phil Havik, for sharing data with us for some years. However, we have, for reasons emphasized above, realized that a consistent long-run dataset is best constructed from scratch to ensure the highest possible degree of comparability across time and space.

We located and photographed most of the raw data we used in the London School of Economics library, the French National Library, the library of Humboldt University of Berlin, the Library of the Italian Chamber of Deputies, and the municipal library of Porto. A large part of the data is also available in digitized PDF format from the British Online Archives, the Gallica digital library for francophone sources, and the IMF archives for the postcolonial period.

The raw data covers more than 4,700 country-year combinations, including more than 130,000 revenue items of which more than 25,000 are unique. An "item" is the most basic revenue unit available, comprising the revenue of a single tax, or sometimes even that of a single taxpayer (e.g., a large mining corporation). These are classified into the broad categories described below. We classify every single item according to modern IMF statistical definitions. In order to ensure a high level of comparability, we classified the items only after all data had been sourced (rather than during the transcription process). This means that an item, say "licenses for businesses," is classified in the same way in country X and country Y.[5]

In order to move beyond nominal aggregates, we deflated revenues using wages for low-skilled workers and normalized them by population, using data from Frankema and Jerven (2014) for the latter step. This leaves us with a panel dataset of consistently coded real revenue categories, comparable across time and space.

Our database focuses on ordinary revenue. A first important classification choice thus pertains to the identification of ordinary vs. extraordinary revenue. The ordinary budget is then further separated into tax and nontax revenue. Tax revenue itself is differentiated into direct, indirect, and trade taxes. In addition, we separate resource revenue as well as we could from these budgets. We do this as consistently as possible, for example, by consulting secondary sources and IMF reports. It is worth noting that, especially when resource revenue is very low, statistical offices tend not to report resource revenues separately in the annual revenue statements. Finally, we aim to identify revenues that were actually received by the exchequer throughout, rather than those amounts merely planned or budgeted. Clearly, actual receipts and budgeted amounts can differ for many reasons.

When coding the taxes, we generally rely on the IMF government finance statistics manual. Direct taxes are those that are directly levied on people and businesses, such as income taxes, head taxes, poll taxes, and profit taxes. However, we also counted business licenses in this category because they are, in principle, nothing but a head tax on businesses (that can vary by type of business). This does not mean, however, that we counted all licenses as direct taxes. Dog license and car license fees are obviously indirect taxes. Finally, grazing fees and land taxes (such as zakat) are counted as direct because they are basically direct taxes when the largest part of the population works in agriculture. The same holds true for fees for fishing rights. Indirect taxes are those levied on all forms of transactions (e.g., VAT and excise taxes) or licenses that are required for purchasing a certain good (e.g., arms licenses).[6] We further differentiate these taxes into trade and non-trade taxes.

Nontax revenue captures revenue from all nontax activities of the state such as revenue from public enterprises, the rental of government assets, and interest on government equities. We are careful to exclude revenue that might have been classified as ordinary by the respective authorities in the historical period, but would be extraordinary by modern accounting standards. This pertains typically to regular transfers from the colonial metropole and sales of assets (e.g., land, stores). The former are transfers that would be classified as aid or grants today, whereas the latter are extraordinary in the sense that they do not recur.

A final important category are resource revenues, which we mark separately from all other revenue independent of the exact way in which they are collected. These range from direct taxes on the profits of resource enterprises, licenses related to resource exploration and exploitation, to dividends from state-owned companies. However, we do not consider this finer disaggregation of resource revenue particularly meaningful. Whether resource revenue is collected through an excess profits tax on a few big state-owned companies, or these gains are simply transferred to the government, is an accounting question that has little economic meaning.

Constructing the Nominal Wage Series for Africa, 1890–2015

The wages we use depict the daily remuneration of unskilled nonagricultural laborers in nominal local currency. This reflects several important considerations. Principally, it is general practice to deflate incomes by the price of consumption goods. For example, the income of a laborer might be deflated by the amount of millet (s)he can buy, that is the purchasing power of their income. States, however, do not consume millet. Instead, one of the principal expenditure items for states in Africa has historically been the wage bill (Gardner, 2012). Therefore, wages can be used to approximate the changing expenses states face. We primarily use *urban* labor, as rural labor markets in most African polities were not very deep at the start of our sample, and because most of the state's activity was concentrated in urban areas. We use *unskilled* labor for a similar reason: skilled labor was very scarce in colonial times, and this category was often monopolized by white settlers. Moreover, skill categories can change over time, whereas unskilled labor is a category with a greater degree of constancy.

For many anglophone countries before 1960, our data comes from the unaltered series on urban laborer compensation assembled by Frankema and van Waijenburg (2012). Exceptions are Egypt, Sudan, and South Africa, for which we used various sources. For francophone and lusophone colonies, we employ official statistical publications issued by the imperial authorities, many of whom report statutory minimum wages or average unskilled wages. To fill the gaps between data points where necessary, we carefully assess whether an interpolation is possible. During the colonial period, this is relatively unproblematic as prices were relatively stable.

As explained in greater detail in the data appendix for our working paper (Albers et al., 2020), for the early postcolonial period, we similarly took the unskilled wage to be the statutory minimum wage. This information was often provided in IMF country reports, which we supplemented with a wide array of secondary, often country-specific, academic studies. Where a regionally differentiated minimum wage existed, we took the simple average of all regions, and we focused on the wage in industry, rather than agriculture, as closest in line with urban wages. A minimum wage did not exist in all countries, in which case we focused on the reported pay in sectors that are predominantly low skilled (e.g., miners or construction workers). In rare cases, the public sector (often a large parastatal sector) was the only employer of substantial size in the formal sector. In these cases, we used wages of the lowest pay scale in the public sector.

Minimum wage scales were no longer adjusted in many countries between the mid-1970s and the late 1990s (Bhorat et al., 2017). This means that the legal minimum wage ceases to be an economically meaningful reference category, as it had not kept up with rapid inflation. From the early 2000s onward, legislation in many countries had (partially) caught up with inflation. From this point on, minimum wage rates (as reported by the International Labour Organization) can often be considered meaningful again.

This leaves us with the task of connecting the meaningful minimum wages in the 2000s with their meaningful counterparts in the 1970s. Given the high inflation rate, a linear interpolation would be clearly impermissible. Instead, we ensure that our urban unskilled daily wages reflect the dynamics of market wages by exploiting information on wage growth in low-skill-intensive sectors such as food processing, wage growth in manufacturing, public sector wages, and price indices (consumer prices and GDP deflators). We take low-skilled and mean industrial wages from data by the United Nations Industrial Development Organization, while consumer prices and public sector wages are supplied in most cases by IMF country reports. We prefer consumer price indices over public sector wages: Empirical evidence for a broad sample of African countries shows that, on average, 70 percent of increases in inflation are passed through to nominal wages in industry (Mazumdar with Mazaheri, 2000). Public sector wages, on the other hand, were often more rigid.

We validate our wage deflator by comparing it to results derived from other deflators. For example, we deflate revenue figures using the GDP deflator from the Penn World Table, and find similar dynamics. Using the more familiar metric of taxes as a share of GDP also leads to similar conclusions as the ones presented here – although we have noted that this metric is not consistently available for much of the colonial period.

The Long-Run Trend in Taxation in African Countries

Figure 4.2 shows our main result: real per capita total revenue, as well as hard-to-collect taxes, averaged for all polities in Africa. As discussed early, the amount of hard-to-collect taxes excludes trade and resource taxes and is interpretable as a measure of fiscal capacity (Besley and Persson, 2014). Two features of Africa's fiscal history stand out immediately. First, during the twentieth century, Africa experienced strong growth in total revenue. Starting from a low level, growth was steady and considerable before World War II. It picked up markedly after the war and again in the early 1970s. Overall, fiscal capacity grew rapidly, and per capita real revenue was eleven times larger in 2000 than it had been in 1900. Although this does not yet allow us to make a statement regarding the levels of African state capacity in comparison to other regions, state capacity was clearly growing at a rapid pace, especially in the second half of the century. Second, revenue from taxation excluding trade and resource taxes also grew markedly, although at a slightly slower pace. This implies that over time, governments in Africa tended to receive a smaller share of revenue from taxes that are hard to collect, but the overall pattern is one of growth in the capacity to collect taxes.

We highlight two main conclusions that can be drawn from this pattern. The first is that the question "why do African countries tax

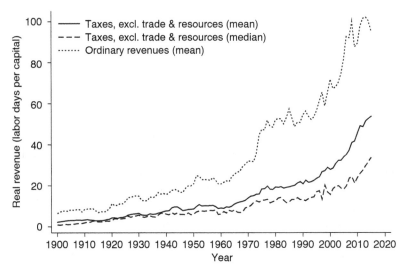

Figure 4.2 Real revenue per capita, Africa, 1900–2015
This figure is also published in Albers et al. (2020, Figure 1a).

so little?" appears to be misguided. Instead of low capacity and stagnation in collection of taxes, the dominant pattern is that of growth and expansion. Our data shows that real total revenue per capita in the average African state has grown strongly since the 1910s.[7] Growth was strong throughout the early period and lasted in terms of both hard-to-collect taxes and total revenue until the very early postcolonial period in the 1960s, when growth paused momentarily. The aggregate pattern was again one of growth from the late 1960s and remained so until a marked negative shock beginning in 1979. We observe decline and stagnation on average in the 1980s, but growth returned in the 1990s and continues right into current times. In this later period, growth has been relatively stronger in ordinary revenue than in direct taxes.

However, such a compressed view averaging data across a whole continent masks two important aspects of variation. The first aspect pertains to the volatility of the growth itself. Fixed-effect panel regressions suggest that the volatility of revenue was negatively associated with the collection of hard-to-collect taxes. The direction of causality is clear in this case: Capacity-building taxes reduced volatility, whereas the reliance on trade and resource taxation increased volatility. This relationship holds true for the whole period, as well as for subsections before and after 1970. This suggests that revenue volatility may be a more salient feature of African states rather than low growth in overall revenue. We thus propose that future research should focus less on any absolute gap in average taxation and GDP per capita between African countries and the rest of the world, and instead study the causes of revenue volatility and the underlying reasons for the heterogeneity of country experiences that this new dataset permits. These findings may seem striking from the perspective of some of the economic literature on taxation, which has principally been occupied with finding reasons why African states have been poor and weak (Acemoğlu and Robinson, 2010). The patterns in the new time series suggest that these are not the right questions.

The second aspect pertains to the variation over time and across countries itself. Slicing the data into different periods, Table 4.3 illustrates the temporal and spatial heterogeneity by considering the unweighted mean of annual growth rates across countries and the standard deviation thereof. As we explore the heterogeneity between the countries elsewhere (Albers et al., 2020), we highlight how these

Table 4.3 *Real growth rates in hard-to-collect taxes and total revenues (percentages)*

| | Real growth of hard-to-collect taxes | | Growth of total ordinary revenue | |
	Mean	Std.	Mean	Std.
1900–14	6.0	15.8	2.4	12.8
World War I	3.1	15.8	0.0	10.6
1919–39	4.3	3.4	3.7	2.8
World War II	2.8	11.0	0.8	7.2
1946–59	0.8	4.5	1.5	3.9
1960–79	4.5	3.9	4.5	3.5
1980–99	2.2	4.0	0.9	3.8
2000–15	5.0	4.4	3.5	3.6

Note: The growth rates in the table represent unweighted averages across the balanced sample of 41 African countries of the fiscal capacity dataset by Albers et al. (2020). The standard deviation is calculated across the sample of the period-specific growth rates.

numbers allow us to substantiate what is known about political history of taxation. The aggregate pattern of growth in revenue in the period 1900–1950 matches the economic growth and expansion referred to as the cash crop revolution and the rise of the marketing boards that collected revenue from these exports (Jerven, 2010b). In areas that were not very prosperous in terms of export receipts, colonial authorities introduced direct taxes earlier in the period (Frankema and van Waijenburg, 2014). More generally, authorities introduced direct taxes across the board in the 1940s.

Growth in total revenue was also visible during the early colonial period because colonial power reached out into the hinterlands of coastal colonies. Authorities gradually expanded an institutional apparatus for collecting "hard taxes" or direct taxes; this was apparent as growth in revenue excluding trade and resource taxes caught up with the growth in total revenue by the 1940s.[8] During the interwar period, colonial states expanded their collection of hard-to-collect taxes, the real proceeds of which grew on average by 4.3 percent. Interestingly, the period of the two world wars comes close to fiscal institution building. During both wars, receipts from hard-to-collect taxes increased significantly, while total ordinary revenue stalled.[9] After World War II, when the expansion of the colonial states increasingly rested on an increase in trade receipts, the share of direct taxes started a long decline and never regained the relative position it had during the war.[10] It is worth underlining the fact that when examining the share of direct taxes in total taxes only, as is sometimes done in the literature, one would conclude that fiscal capacity in many African countries has been receding since the war. Measured by real revenue, however, the story is one of growth over the long run.

After independence, growth picked up again after a brief period of stagnation during decolonization in the 1960s. After this period, trade taxes increased significantly. This matches the familiar story that the postcolonial developmental states used taxes on exports to finance an expanded state and investment in industrial capacity (Austin et al., 2017). Our data show that trade taxes were the mainstay of public finances in Africa throughout the century, reaching a peak during the early independence period in 1970. Concurrent with this compositional shift, total revenue picks up in real terms, partly due to a growth in resource revenue.

The 1980s were a period of crisis for African fiscal states; real revenue collapsed across the board. Total revenue was most affected when African states reduced their collection of taxes on trade as they implemented liberalization policies.[11] Revenue recovered at the end of the century, largely driven by an expansion in indirect taxes such as value-added taxes (Ahlerup et al. 2014). Overall, growth in total revenue and tax extraction was higher in the colonial period than it was under independent African governments, although this trend masks the large weight of the downturn in the 1980s for the latter period. If we exclude the 1980s, growth rates look similar for both eras.

Lessons Learned

The main message is quite simple. The lack of time-series data on taxation in Africa has meant that the dominant focus has been on explaining the very important but perhaps too reductive question of why some less developed poor countries are taxing so little in comparison with rich countries today. The focus has been on explaining this "today" because we have lacked time-series data. Our new dataset will allow researchers to test much more nuanced explanations, particularly of patterns of longitudinal change. The fact that previous datasets have relied on nominal figures or ratios of revenue to GDP has not only limited the scope of investigation longitudinally but has also hampered the reliability of cross-country comparisons, since error margins in GDP levels have been considered to be at least in the range of plus or minus 50 percent (Jerven, 2010c, 2014).

The primary lesson we have drawn from the new dataset is that it challenges the orthodoxy of stagnation. While in the past researchers have focused on explaining low and stagnant levels of taxation, our new time-series data shows that African fiscal systems have experienced decades of growth. Another important lesson is that growth has fluctuated. The dataset opens up new avenues of investigation and allows for more sophisticated testing of hypotheses about historical trajectories in state development in the twentieth century.

The lessons learned here lean toward supporting concerns raised in the early growth regression literature that the variables used to capture policy and politics were static and showed no change (such as in the open-versus-closed typology), whereas economic variables were highly volatile. The authors of that literature worried that if averages were used in the regression, one could "falsely attribute externally-induced adversity to policy" (Easterly et al., 1993: 474). By extension, the same argument and warning applies to the practice of using present-day outcomes to test for the importance of historical variables. As our new dataset establishes, concerns about such practices are warranted, and it is clear that economic and political change – the conjectural element – was important to such an extent that the persistence of "weak" African states appears at times to be questionable. Change and growth are the salient features of taxation and development in Africa, not stasis and stagnation.

5 | *Wages and Poverty: From Roots of Poverty to Trajectories of Living Standards*

One of the main themes of this book is how the availability of evidence has shaped narratives. Accounts of poverty in Africa that center on numbers have been particularly limited by the availability of evidence. Although the historical scholarship on poverty in Africa is rich, the representation of poverty in Africa has been dominated by the World Bank data See Jerven 2018b.

Poverty has a long history in Africa, yet the most influential narrative of African poverty spans a short period. The history of poverty as told by World Bank numbers starts in the 1980s with the first Living Standards Measurement Surveys. This history is also a very narrow one. There is a disconnect between the theoretical and historical under-pinnings of how we understand and define poverty in Africa and how it has been quantified in practice. While it is generally agreed that poverty is multidimensional and has certain aspects that are specific to time and location, the shorthand for poverty in the literature is the dollar-per-day metric.

In popular and contemporary debates, "poverty" and "Africa" are sometimes presented as intimately linked. Yet this direct association is relatively recent.[1] In the 1970s, when Anthony Hopkins wrote his *Economic History of West Africa* (1973), the myth he had to dispel was that of "Merry Africa," whereas in 2009 he reflected on how Africa was depicted as a continent of poverty, as in the "Make Poverty History" campaign of 2005 (Hopkins, 2009). The starting point of analysis of African economic growth and poverty tends to be that growth in Africa has chronically failed and that poverty is persistent. This does not match up with the work of African historians, who have long argued that peasant producers and workers were relatively prosperous from 1940 to 1970.[2] This narrative is not completely unknown to economists, as Bourguignon and Morrisson (2002: 739) found using a large database of compiled household surveys. They note that "in 1950 12 percent of world inhabitants with incomes less than median lived in Africa. By 1992, 30 percent did." Yet these changes in poverty over time have had little influence on how the history of poverty in Africa by numbers is told. At one level, historical vantage point plays a role. Recent and contemporary events loom large and frame research questions. Although relative prosperity in Africa was commonplace in the 1970s, it has proven easy to lose track of these comparative data points in the midst of the "Africa Growth Tragedy" (Easterly and Levine, 1997) or the "Lost Decades" of the 1980s and 1990s (Easterly, 2001).

A main contributing factor to the ahistorical approach to poverty is the availability of quantitative evidence on poverty. The problem is that in mainstream economic analysis, what constitutes relevant data points has been limited to World Bank surveys of poverty. Once we widen the scope of evidence, the approach to understanding poverty in the Africa might change considerably.

Economic historians have long emphasized the importance of the African economic past for enriching contemporary economic analysis (Hopkins, 1986; Manning, 1987). Patrick Manning warned in the 1980s that "future work in African economic history will be conditioned fundamentally by the limits on available data, and by the success or failure of projects to generate or systematize further data" (Manning, 1987, 55). While Manning did not subscribe to a narrow interpretation of data,[3] I think he was referring to datasets that can be easily used by other scholars as a way of stimulating further work. In the same survey article, he suggested that the key reason that African economic history was not discussed at economics meetings was the lack of availability of such datasets.

This chapter presents data that has been published and collated in the past decade and discusses how that data changes our interpretation of poverty in Africa in the twentieth century. It briefly assesses the stock of knowledge about poverty rates and levels in sub-Saharan Africa since the 1980s. This is important because a misunderstanding in the literature seems to overrate the quality of contemporary evidence and underrate the quality of historical evidence. This false appreciation of data quality has meant that the history of poverty by numbers is very short. More generally, the lack of long time-series data on growth and poverty has caused what Austin (2008) refers to as a "compression of history." How economic historians of Africa have responded to the compression of history is the topic of the second half of the chapter, but first it is worth diagnosing the knowledge problem that caused that compression.

Historical and Contemporary Data on Poverty and Growth

The availability and the character of poverty numbers and economic statistics have shaped historical analysis of poverty and growth in sub-Saharan Africa. Quantitative economic histories of economic growth are written using time-series data on economic growth. In this case, "Year 1" has been 1960 and hence economists have focused on the postcolonial period.[4] Those who write histories of poverty using the dollar-per-day metric use 1990 as "Year 1." Both are artificial starting points, but data availability limits us to this time frame and restricts what kinds of questions can be investigated.

The narratives of economic growth in African economies change dramatically when we reject the starting point of 1960. Notions such as "chronic growth failure" and the "bottom billion" would not hold if we abandoned the short time horizon.[5] Similarly, narratives of trends in living standards in Africa are shaped by the current configuration of what constitutes poverty knowledge at the World Bank. The short history of poverty by numbers in Africa is misleading because it fails to contextualize the poverty of the 1990s and 2000s in a longer time perspective.

The dearth of immediately available data on trajectories of poverty has led researchers to take shortcuts when studying long-term historical roots of poverty in Africa. Instead of carefully outlining the trajectory of economic growth or poverty over past centuries, the economic literature is content to treat GDP per capita today as standing in for lack of growth in the past. Thus, according to this method, if you can correlate the income distribution today with some explanatory variable in the past, you have found the historical roots of Africa's relative poverty.

Fenske (2010a: 4) claimed that this "new African economic history," a term Hopkins (2009) coined, was "causal history," noting that "practitioners of causal history focus on identifying causal historical relationships, which sets them apart from the qualitative 'old' economic historians and from much of the 'new' economic history." Presenting new econometric history as causal history and setting aside old, non-econometric history as noncausal amounts to a blanket statement about methodological superiority. At the very least, the methodologies of both economics and history are necessary if one is to grasp the causes of poverty.[6] Privileging one over the other can only lead to misconceptions and most certainly leads us down a road where we actively ignore knowledge. John Iliffe's approach to poverty in *The African Poor: A history* (1987)[7] argues that because poverty is multidimensional, it defies simple quantification and advanced econometric testing.[8] He argues that the two types of poverty he identifies – structural and conjunctural – have different causes and trend lines. This nuanced understanding of poverty is lost in the quantitative methods of the "new economic history of Africa." Iliffe used historical observations of poverty in Africa to identify plausible patterns of causality but did not apply tests of statistical causality to his theories. This is a pragmatic solution to dealing with the type of the evidence available. If the usefulness of evidence were determined by what kind of statistical test can be used, such information about poverty would be discarded because it is not directly comparable with poverty metrics used today (Iliffe, 1987: 143). Iliffe's approach looks at evidence for what it tells us, not for how compatible it is with contemporary methodologies.

Iliffe highlighted the inadequacy of numerical sources as one of the key obstacles in the study of African poverty. Cautioning against an overreliance on oral traditions and generalized descriptions, Iliffe suggests that records of poverty in documents such as missionaries' letters, travelers' journals, and administrators' reports might be the best alternative (Iliffe, 1987: 2–3). To that list one could add information that can be obtained through the meticulous study of population censuses from the colonial period (Fetter, 1987). In *A History of African Motherhood* (2013), Rhiannon Stephens also shows how oral sources can complement linguistic and archeological evidence. Citing a lack of written data, especially before 1860, Stephens uses a mixture of these sources (and others) to help reveal the social, political, and economic history of African motherhood. Those whose study of poverty is limited to and by numbers miss significant parts of the story of African history when they overlook other types of sources.

The study of historical trajectories of growth and poverty in sub-Saharan Africa has been limited by the databases, and this is especially the case for the history of poverty. First, there has been a change from appreciating the multidimensionality of poverty to using the term "poverty" as shorthand for a very specific monetary measure.

An example is the World Bank's world poverty headcount. In principle, the poverty headcount is a universal measure of how many people (in absolute terms or as a proportion of the population) do not have enough income to cover a basket of subsistence goods.[9] If the poverty problem had been conceived as a relative measure that reflected country inequality, the global discourse on poverty would have been radically different.

The use of numbers in social sciences is usually justified because it adds rigor and reliability, but on closer inspection the poverty numbers are not nearly as credible as they are often purported to be. The global number is based on small (or nonexistent) samples at the local level. In Africa, household surveys covering a few thousand households are conducted infrequently and in only some of the countries (Serajuddin et al., 2015). Our ability to collect consistent data on poverty is constrained by problems with both design and implementation.

In the current methodology, if you want to know about poverty levels in any given country, it will cost about US $1 million and take from two to three years from start to finish (Jerven, 2017). Once the survey data are available, the first step is to use foreign exchange rates to express the income of one country in the currency of another. However, differences in domestic prices on nontradable goods cause a divergence in purchasing power parity (PPP) (Taylor and Taylor, 2004). To achieve PPP, one needs to adjust for the fact that one dollar goes a lot further in a country like Burundi than it does in a country like Belgium. This entails a complicated process of collecting local prices, weighting them appropriately, then constructing a basket of goods and services for each country and comparing their costs (Deaton and Heston, 2010).

Since 1970, the World Bank has conducted eight International Comparison Program rounds; the most recent was in 2011 (World Bank, n.d.). Participation from African countries has been uneven in these rounds. In the 1970 and 1973 rounds, only Kenya participated. In 1980, Kenya was joined by Malawi and Zambia, and by 1993, the number of participating countries had increased to cover more than half the continent.[10] Only eleven of forty-eight sub-Saharan African countries have completed regular studies that measure living standards. If you widen the scope to include other types of poverty surveys, you will find that as of 2012, only twenty-five of forty-eight countries had at least two surveys that could be used for tracking poverty trends over the past decade. In the remaining twenty-three countries, there is not enough information to say something about the direction of change. For five countries that represent 5 percent of the African population, there is no data for measuring poverty at all (Beegle et al., 2016). Beyond availability of data, there are questions of sampling, survey design, and various types of measurement errors that weaken the view that the poverty numbers are of a quality that justifies the very strong role they have in motivating research questions and shaping conventional wisdom about "poverty."[11]

Because the study of poverty excludes these alternative sources of information from consideration, the history of poverty that is being analyzed is foreshortened. A perspective on the history of poverty in Africa that focuses on numbers and particularly on money is particularly limiting because it explicitly leaves some information out. This is true from the perspective of econometricians, for whom the availability of quantitative evidence represents the boundary of investigation. Thus, one way of driving the literature forward is to extend the quantitative horizon backward.

Extending the History of Poverty by Numbers: New Evidence

Because historical numbers on poverty are scarce, many of the "historical" papers use evidence from a very recent past (Jerven, 2010c). However, a "renaissance of African Economic History" has stimulated a wave of new archival research that seeks to measure poverty and living standards, particularly for the colonial period (Austin and Broadberry, 2014). As was emphasized in the chapter presenting the GDP estimates, observations are still indicative rather than definitive and conclusive. The previous section might be summarized as saying that our knowledge about poverty by numbers in the recent postcolonial period is overrated. What follows suggests that our knowledge of trends in "poverty" or, at the very least, in "living standards" in the colonial period might be underrated.

Living Standards and Real Wages

A real wages series is the cost of goods that workers consumed at a given time. Those who create such series compile price data into a bare-bone subsistence basket of goods: the absolute minimum daily requirements for an adult male.[12] They collect historical prices from a variety of sources to calculate how much the basket would have cost at any given time and compare the cost of that basket to the nominal wages an unskilled laborer would have earned at that time. Standardizing income and needs in this way makes comparisons of well-being over both time and distance possible. Frankema and van Waijenburg (2011) use this approach in their analysis of living standards in eight British African colonies from 1880 to 1940. They argue that real wages exceeded subsistence levels for this period and that wages in a selection of the colonies studied actually exceeded those in major Asian cities. They emphasize that a divergence of paths has occurred not only between Africa and those comparable Asian locations but also within the African continent. They point to the different paths that led to present-day poverty and challenge the argument that colonial institutions and path dependency are at the root of poverty in sub-Saharan Africa.[13]

Their article specifically addresses what they perceive to be a central claim of the literature: That African poverty has been persistent over time because of structural impediments to growth. Researchers disagree about what the root cause of lack of growth and persistent poverty is but take it as given that Africa has failed. Yet Frankema and van Waijenburg's (2011) real wage data on former British colonies show that real wages in urban areas grew steadily from the 1880s into the 1960s and that in some periods and some locations this growth was very rapid. In British West Africa, annual average growth typically varied from 2 to 3 percent, but sometimes the growth rate was even higher. There was growth throughout East and Southern Africa, but at a lower rate of from 1 to 2 percent annually.

Using similar evidence but not the same subsistence baskets, Bowden et al. (2008) compiled wage data, poverty data, and real wage data for three settler economies (South Africa, Zimbabwe, and Kenya) and three peasant economies (Ethiopia, Uganda, and Ghana) and compared long-term trends in trajectories and levels of living standards. They challenge the thesis of Acemoğlu et al. (2001, 2002) that suggests that higher levels of European settlement led to more productive institutions, that those institutions in turn predict better economic outcomes today, and that higher levels of poverty, in particular lower wages, were observed in the settler economies.

Bowden et al.'s investigation shows that real wages stagnated in the settler economies, whereas in the peasant economies (Uganda and Ghana), real wages rose markedly from the 1910s into the 1970s (2008). These datasets allow for a long-term historical reading of poverty in Africa and raise questions about viewing poverty as an "African" structural problem. Rönnbäck's (2014) analysis of living standards, which uses wages from commercial records in the precolonial Gold Coast, supports Bowden et al.'s analysis. Borrowing again from Iliffe (1987), it may be more appropriate to view the high incidence of poverty as a conjunctural problem from the 1980s onward.

Anthropometrics and Living Standards

Another method used to measure poverty draws on anthropometrics. Researchers have used mean adult height as a measure of well-being. That is because height is a measure of the physical quality of life, in particular the quantity and quality of childhood nutrition, housing, sanitation, and medical care. We know that stunted adult height is a result of inadequate access to essential resources in childhood (Moradi, 2009: 723–724). This method preempts the critique that genetics impact height by using average population height. When one aggregates to the population level, the influence of genetics is cancelled out and is irrelevant for comparisons over time for one population (Austin et al., 2007). Moradi (2009) suggests that the genetic pool can be assumed to be fairly constant at the macro level, given the relatively short period of time that such studies typically focus on.

Using average height as a measure for quality of life has several advantages. First, because height is an outcome of well-being (rather than an input, like income), this method does not discriminate between different types of input (which avoids the need to standardize consumption baskets) or make any assumptions about basic minimum requirements. The primary point of interest is whether an individual's condition was sufficient to meet their needs. Further, height measures are applicable to the diverse socioeconomic conditions of developing countries (hunters, pastoralists, subsistence farmers, urban laborers) and thus facilitate comparison across groups. Mean height is also sensitive to inequality. Because of the diminishing returns of nutritional input on height, redistribution from rich to poor will raise the mean population measure. Finally, the height data allows for statistical insight into historical periods for which other measures of poverty are lacking (Moradi, 2008: 1109–1110).

Such methods are generally restricted to relative measures of well-being. It compares mean adult heights for different birth cohorts. If one group has a greater mean height than the other, the researcher assumes that well-being increased through an improvement in overall well-being, a reduction of inequality, or both. The most readily available height data before the existence of regular survey data are typically found in documents associated with the slave trade or colonial armies. Of course, these samples are not random and they may not always be representative. A preference for physically fit (taller) slaves could skew the sample mean, and military enlistment was often voluntary, paid, and subject to minimum height requirements.

It is important for researchers to have an intimate familiarity with their dataset and with the dynamics of the region(s) they are analyzing. Considerable attention is generally dedicated to demonstrating that the dataset is either representative of the broader population or that econometric techniques can and have corrected it to be so. For example, in their analysis of Dutch recruits born in Ghana and Burkina Faso in the period 1800 to 1840, Austin et al. (2012) suggest that because the recruits in their dataset were mostly purchased from slaveowners, bias associated with volunteering was unlikely. Further, they find no evidence of a height premium (overrepresentation from genetically taller regions) and thus dismiss the idea that a sample of slaves would be taller on average than the general population from which it was drawn. After correcting for the effect of regional origin and minimum height requirements, Austin et al. (2012) compared average heights with those in other regions of the world and found that people in Ghana and Burkina Faso are further behind today than they were 200 years ago.

Austin et al. (2007), who analyzed regional inequality in Ghana from 1880 to 2000, found that living standards improved during colonial times and then regressed after the economic crisis of the 1970s. They used data from a variety of times and sources. First, they used attestation forms to estimate average heights for those born from the 1880s to the 1920s. To account for minimum height requirements, they applied truncated regressions using a maximum likelihood estimator in order to establish mean heights that are closer to representative for the population. They then compared these averages with data taken from the 1987–1988 Ghana Living Standards Survey and demographic health surveys from 1988, 1993, 1998–1999, and 2003 in order to evaluate the development of regional differences in Ghana over time.

Moradi (2008, 2009) followed a similar methodology in his refutation of the notion that contemporary poverty is rooted in colonial legacies. Using records from colonial armies, he argued that Ghana and Kenya experienced significant improvements in health and well-being as measured by average population height. He compared improvements in this metric with data from other developing countries to demonstrate that Ghana and Kenya were outperforming comparable international countries during colonial times (1920s to 1970s).

It is worth emphasizing that the observed increases in mean heights in populations living in regions and colonies that were experiencing increases in export revenues from the late nineteenth century into the 1970s provides strong corroborative evidence that underlines the positive trend observed in other indicators. Taken alone, one might see export growth and worry about trends in other "invisible" sectors. If one sees increases in real wages, one might still worry about sampling and distribution. These findings together may indicate a more positive and lasting impact of the "cash crop revolution" than was previously thought. However, work on distribution and income inequality is still in progress and we might learn more as further datasets on wages from Francophone and Lusophone Africa become available.[14]

Conclusion

It is understandable that the international datasets on growth and poverty have shaped the literature and conventional wisdom. The perceived credibility of international numbers and their comparability have meant that they are far more accessible than the colonial ledgers, commercial accounts, and army recruiting forms that newer studies have drawn from. Some of the data such as the colonial blue books are now available online, contain standardized information, and are thus easy to use. One reason researchers have used such sources in conjunction with other sources is perhaps a justifiable worry that using these sources exclusively would essentially retell the story of progress colonial administrators constructed. One writes African history from the imperial archives with serious caveats about the content of the sources.

Yet the lack of data from before 1960 has led to a "compression of history." The methodology used to make correlations between present-day poverty and historical factors has had a strong appeal in economic studies. In addition, the lack of long time-series data made it easier to act as if little or nothing happened between a long-ago point and the present day.

When historians encounter a high degree of methodological bias from researchers in the discipline of economics, they may be tempted to ignore numerical evidence and favor alternative sources of knowledge. However, one should be careful not to draw a line in the sand between quantitative and nonquantitative studies of poverty or between quantitative methods and historical analysis in general. When Stephens (2013) wrote her history of motherhood in Uganda, which covers a long time period, she faced the source availability constraints we would expect, particularly in the period before 1800. Her approach is instructive. She is aware that her oral history records may be biased, but she seeks to corroborate the oral history findings with linguistic evidence, particularly with the use of lexicostatistics. Thus, her method uses many types of fragmented historical evidence instead of telling a story that relies on quantitative or qualitative methods alone. In a similar vein, this chapter seeks to encourage studies that use a multitude of historical methods to query current assumptions and lengthen the historical perspective on the incidence of poverty in Africa. The dominant narrative on poverty in Africa is number-centric, but it did not have to be that way. It is striking now to think that in the recent past there was general acceptance of the idea that poverty was multidimensional and that the poor had a say in defining what constituted poverty. In the 1990s, inspired by the work of Robert Chambers (1997), the World Bank sponsored a research project called "Voices of the Poor" that collected different types of data on the experiences of poor people around the world (Narayan et al., 2000). This research was largely swept aside as the dollar-a-day measure was codified as "poverty" in the adoption of the UN's Millennium Development Goals.

Partly conditioned by the availability of data, the overwhelming tendency in the mainstream economic literature has been to offer an explanation for the relative poverty of African economies vis-à-vis the West and other emerging regions. This has only been possible through the appearance of imagined and stylized facts about Africa. Imagined facts derive from the economic growth literature that in the 1990s began focusing on explaining slow growth in Africa. The imagined event that arose from this focus is a chronic failure of economic growth in Africa. The combination of the short time series and the use of data on average growth in the postcolonial period (1965–1995) produced analyses that ignored periods of higher growth in the 1950s, 1960s, and 1970s and again from the late 1990s into the 2000s and 2010s and sought to find an explanation for growth in Africa that was unduly colored by the lower growth in the 1980s (Jerven, 2015). When one uses datasets or at the very least strong supporting information that document growth from at least since the 1910s, such a perspective does not stand the test of time (Jerven, 2010b, 2014b). The frame of "chronic failure" was embodied in the phrase "bottom billion." In the literature of the 2000s, the task of explaining slow growth was gradually conflated with the task of explaining low GDP per capita "today." At some level, low income "today" could mean no growth "yesterday," but that is a testable (yet untested) hypothesis and has proven to be a shaky foundation for a literature that purports to explain the historical roots of poverty. Another level of conflation happened when researchers approached poverty as "absolute deprivation" and conflated high poverty today with low GDP per capita today.

Some of the evidence reviewed in this chapter points to newer stylized facts. One is that the "gap" in living standards between African and non-African economies was probably lower a century or two ago. Corroborating evidence indicates that the incidence of poverty was not a typical African phenomenon five decades ago. Thus, enriching the database with new historical estimates offers comparative frames other than the ones we are used to from the contemporary literature. Moreover, the study of longer-term trajectories in growth, poverty, wages, and other metrics that capture living standards indicates a long trend of improvement from the 1910s into the 1970s in most African economies.

This raises the possibility that the 1980s were a historical anomaly. This information may offer a better perspective from which to reach a historical comparative verdict on the "Africa rising" narrative. First, there is nothing new about growth in African economies. Second, since the evidence that economic growth led to poverty reduction in the recent period is weak (Organization for Economic Cooperation and Development, 2013), the period of growth and poverty reduction since the late 1990s may compare unfavorably to growth in the 1960s or even in the colonial period.

6 | Conclusion

The new African economic history used econometric methods and quantitative data to make big claims about the causes of Africa's current relative poverty vis-à-vis the rest of the world, especially the wealthy countries in the West. At first historians did not respond to these claims, as Hopkins (2009) pointed out, while African economic historians tended to warn about the "compression of history" (Austin, 2009). This book has sought to summarize some of my own research and that of many other economic historians whose research has contributed to a decompression of history by providing long-term historical time series on some of the central metrics of economic development: wages, poverty, living standards, taxation, and economic growth.

I have drawn conclusions about these trends in the individual chapters. All claims are of course subject to doubts about the data quality and by the fact that a lot of data are simply missing. However, the aggregate trends for the majority of the countries for the twentieth century is clear, and since they are substantiated by independent sources of evidence it now seems inescapable that the framing of the African development experience in the twentieth century as failed, stagnant, or simply a tragedy is incorrect. The declines of the late twentieth century (from the late 1970s into the early 1990s) wiped out some of the gains made in the rest of the twentieth century, but it seems that the decline of those two decades also gave scholars a frame that has been hard to get rid of.

A central reason why the frame of African failure has stuck with us so persistently is data availability. The research on poverty did not engage with change on the longitudinal dimension but drew upon the availability of data on absolute poverty in Africa from the 1990s. This meant that "Africa" and "poverty" became intertwined, and researchers did not take into account the gains made in the earlier twentieth century. The absolute poverty framing of the 1990s similarly extended to the literature on taxation data, which took simple cross-country observations from "today" that indicated that states in Africa were taxing at low rates. The longer time series shows that this framing has limited validity.

Economic growth data are available back to the 1960s. I have argued elsewhere that averaging out the increases in the 1960s and 1970s by the declines in the 1980s meant that the rise-and-fall feature of African economic development was sidelined in favor of a framing permanent stagnation (Jerven, 2015). I do not argue that explaining the gap in GDP per capita between rich and poor countries today is not a relevant approach at times, but if we do not take on board the fact that these so-called failed countries did indeed grow for decades, we run the risk of underemphasizing the external forces that shape economic development and overemphasizing the insufficiencies of states and policy mistakes. New GDP estimates for the early twentieth century show that growth has been the norm in Africa and the decline in the 1980s was the exception.

The rise of a "new African economic history" has been inspired by cross-country comparisons where Africa stands in as the "failed continent." The dangers are not only that such work degrades Africa as the place where things do not work but also that it uplifts the North as the place where everything works and sweeps away the idiosyncrasies in the workings of societies in the so-called developed countries, thus allowing ourselves to be blinded by our particular historical vantage point.

In 1973, Hopkins highlighted this feature of approaching economic development in African countries: "Accordingly, an understanding of Africa's relative economic backwardness should be sought, not by measuring the continent towards an unrealised ideal, but by identifying specific constraints that limited, in my formulation, the extent of the market" (Hopkins, 2020). Whatever the formulation, the general lesson is clear. The economic history of Africa needs to be studied in its own right.

I have summarized some major efforts that have done so. The focus here has been on the colonial and postcolonial periods, as the main point has been to report on the work on piecing together long-run continuous times-series data on economic change. Research has in the past decades focused on the colonial period, in contrast with the early focus on the precolonial period. The scope for putting together a continuous time series for the precolonial period is limited, but there are certainly opportunities to harmonize data for some times and places, and such studies can be important and settle big questions in the literature. The best examples of such studies that I am aware are provided by Robin Law (1992) and John Thornton (1977). Law tackles the eminently testable question as to whether prices responded to demand and supply in precolonial periods, and documents that indeed it did. Thornton makes use of church records to provide population estimates for Kongo, 1550–1750, and finds that contrary to the thesis that population loss was dramatic in the late precolonial period, his estimates indicate a much more stable population.

This book is not the final word. My purpose is to summarize the grand aggregate features that now emerge as instructive for future research now that the important work of extending the time-series data on central development metrics has been completed. The chief contribution here is to offer a new description of the poverty and wealth of African states in the twentieth century. I have not sought to offer new explanations or reject old causal explanations (such as whether settler colonies did well, or countries with high linguistic fractionalization did poorly); I have simply suggested that new descriptions call for new analysis. We can now study divergent or convergent trajectories on the African continent or vis-à-vis the rest of the world.

A final word of caution. The chapter on seeing like an African state makes it abundantly clear that the quantitative databases do not include many features of African development. New work has made some of these development patterns visible, but many aspects remain invisible. In my own scholarship, I have not only emphasized the lack of numbers and how this have shaped explanations but also that the existing numbers are weak and are of limited use. For instance, the downside of extending the GDP series to the early twentieth century is that a reductive approach to economic development now embraces the whole twentieth century rather than just the second half. The new data series my colleagues and I have constructed does tell us something else about economic development in African countries, but it does not tell us everything.

Appendix to Chapter 3

Agricultural output is estimated by an agricultural demand function with the same parameters that have been used widely in the literature. It could be that our results are sensitive to the calibration. Therefore real GDP per capita is estimated for each country again using two alternative sets of parameters. The third column of Table 3.25 reports the baseline results, where the own-price, income, and cross-price elasticities are set to $e = -0.6$, $g = 0.5$, and $b = 0.1$, respectively. The fourth column shows the results for $e = -0.5$, $g = 0.4$, and $b = 0.1$, as in Malanima (2011). The fifth column reports results for $e = 0.5$, $g = 0.4$, and $b = 0.1$, as in Prados de la Escosura (2012). As the table shows, the average (μ) and standard deviation (σ) of real GDP per capita growth are not materially affected by the choice of parameters.

While Chapter 3 sets out the blueprint for constructing the historical national accounts, this appendix outlines the departures from that blueprint that were needed to deal with differences in data availability from country to country and with other country-specific information.

Gambia (1920–1942)

Three adjustments were necessary in the case of Gambia. First, wages in industry were not reported from 1928. I assumed that wages in this sector grew in line with a weighted average of wage growth in agriculture and services. Second, the blue books note that there were no mines. As a result, industrial output consisted solely of building and manufacturing for this period. Third, no information was recorded on transport output. I assumed that it grew in line with the output of services that were recorded.

To weight our index of wages, I calculated shares of total employment for agriculture, industry, and services, which were based on the 1931

Table 3.25 *Robustness to alternative calibration (percent)*

Country	Sample	$e = -0.6,$ $g = 0.5,$ $b = 0.1$		$e = -0.5,$ $g = 0.4,$ $b = 0.1$		$e = 0.5,$ $g = 0.4,$ $b = 0.1$	
		σ		σ		μ	σ
Gambia	1920–42	−0.9	16.7	−1.2	17.4	−1.5	18.5
Ghana	1900–39	3.6	8.3	3.8	8.4	3.9	8.7
Kenya	1926–46	3.8	9.3	3.7	9.0	3.7	8.9
Malawi	1920–38	2.5	7.5	2.5	6.9	2.5	6.3
Nigeria	1900–40	1.9	10.5	1.9	9.5	1.9	8.6
Sierra Leone	1900–38	4.9	11.2	4.9	11.3	5.0	11.8
Tanzania	1922–37	5.8	7.6	5.6	6.8	5.4	6.1
Uganda	1906–45	2.0	8.2	2.0	7.2	2.0	6.2

Source: Author's calculations based on Blue Book data, Malanima (2011), and Prados de las Escosura (2012).

Report and Summary of the Census of the Gambia (Colony of the Gambia 1932).

Ghana (1900–1939)

There were two caveats to the estimates for Ghana. First, agricultural wages were not reported before 1925. I therefore spliced the aggregate wage index back from 1925 using a weighted average of wages in industry and services. Second, the blue books did not record the exports of class I and class II goods separately after 1932. As a result, I extrapolated using total exports.

To weight our index of wages, I calculated shares of total employment for agriculture, industry, and services, which were based on Aboagye and Bolt (2018).

Kenya (1926–1946)

No departures from the blueprint were necessary for Kenya other than for the calculation of employment shares. The 1931 *Report on the Census Enumeration of the Non-Native Population Made in the Colony and Protectorate of Kenya* (Kenya Colony and Protectorate

1932) only recorded the nonnative population, as the title suggests. As the nonnative population was a tiny fraction of the total population, I used an average of the Gambian, Ghanaian, and Nigerian occupational shares to weight the wage index.

Malawi (1920–1938)

The blue books for Malawi are missing mining output from 1920 to 1924 and 1936 to 1938. Mining is unlikely to have been significant in these years, as just £70 was produced on average in the years for which data exist. Therefore, I spliced the industrial production index backward to 1920 and forward to 1938 using the growth of building and manufacturing output.

The 1931 *Report on the Census* (Nyasaland Protectorate, 1932) for the Nyasaland Protectorate recorded the "Asiatic," and "European" population. As the native population was not recorded, which accounted for virtually the entire population, I used an average of the Gambian, Ghanaian, and Nigerian occupational shares to weight our index of wages.

Nigeria (1900–1940)

In order to move from agricultural consumption to production, data are needed on the net exports of agricultural (class 1 and class 2) goods. Before 1914, the blue books did not break down imports and exports by class. Therefore, based on the level of imports and exports of these goods in 1914, I spliced back using the growth rate in total imports and exports. In 1914, class 1 and class 2 goods made up 92 percent of total exports, which suggests that this assumption is reasonable.

Mining output was not consistently recorded in the blue books before 1920. Therefore, I constructed two industrial production indices, one for 1920–1940 based on the output of all three branches, and one for 1900–1920 based on building and manufacturing. Using the index based on all three branches, I spliced backward from 1920 using the growth rate of the index based on building and manufacturing.

Before 1914, the number of banks listed in the blue books is for southern Nigeria only. However, there is no jump in 1913, which suggests that all of the Nigerian banks were based in the south.

The deflator for industry is a weighted average of the price indices for building, mining, and manufacturing. As mining output is not available before 1920, it follows that a deflator cannot be constructed. Therefore, I projected the industrial deflator backward from 1920 using the growth rate of the building and manufacturing price index.

To weight our index of wages, I calculated shares of total employment for agriculture, industry, and services, which were based on the 1931 *Census of Nigeria* (Government of Nigeria, 1933).

Sierra Leone (1900–1938)

No adjustments were necessary for Sierra Leone other than for the calculation of employment shares. The 1931 *Report of Census* (Sierra Leone, 1931) only recorded the colony and the area surrounding Freetown; it did not record the protectorate. Given that the colony constituted a small fraction of the total population and that there may have been important differences in the occupational structure between the colony and the protectorate, I used an average of the Gambian, Ghanaian, and Nigerian occupational shares to weight the wage index.

Tanzania (1922–1937)

No deviations from the blueprint were necessary for Tanzania other than for the calculation of employment shares. The 1931 *Report on the Non-Native Census* (Tanganyika Territory, 1932) only recorded the nonnative population, as the title implies. As the nonnative population was a small fraction of the total population, I used an average of the Gambian, Ghanaian, and Nigerian occupational shares to weight the wage index.

Uganda (1906–1945)

Due to a number of deficiencies in the blue books for Uganda, a few departures from the baseline were necessary. First, due to inconsistent trade statistics, I assumed that net exports of agricultural goods were zero, which implies that agricultural consumption equaled production, as in Álvarez-Nogal and Prados de la Escosura (2013), Broadberry et al. (2015), and Malanima (2011). Second, mining output was not recorded consistently before 1929. For this reason, I spliced the all-branch index of industrial production backward from this point using a weighted average of the building and manufacturing indices. Third, transport output was not sufficiently recorded before 1924. Therefore, I spliced the all-branch index of services output back from 1924 using a narrower index that excludes transport.

The 1931 *Census Returns* (Uganda Protectorate, 1933) for Uganda only covered the "European," "Indian," "Goan," "Arab," and "other non-native" populations. As the native population was not recorded, which was roughly 90 percent of the total population and presumably had a different occupational structure from that of the nonnative population, I used an average of the Gambian, Ghanaian, and Nigerian occupational shares to weight our index of wages.

Table 3.26 *Commodities*

Good	Agricultural/Industrial
Beans	Agricultural
Beef	Agricultural
Butter	Industrial
Candles	Industrial
Cassava	Agricultural
Coal	Industrial
Cotton	Industrial
Ghee	Industrial
Groundnuts	Agricultural
Kerosene	Industrial
Maize	Agricultural
Matama	Agricultural
Millet	Agricultural
Mutton	Agricultural
Palm oil	Industrial
Potatoes	Agricultural
Rice	Agricultural
Salt	Industrial
Simsim	Agricultural
Soap	Industrial
Sugar	Industrial
Sweet potatoes	Agricultural
Wheat	Agricultural
Yams	Agricultural

Notes

Introduction

1. A case could have been made for including new work on human capital, particularly on the spread of literacy and the role of missionaries. For a review, see Jedwab et al. (2018).

1 A New Economic History for Africa?

1. For a classic statement of the debate, see Fogel and Elton (1983).
2. For a short description, see "Annual meeting of the AEHN: An introduction," at www.aehnetwork.org/conference.
3. Gareth Austin noted in his 2013 Fage Lecture that while we in 2004 could fit the whole active discipline into a minibus, we now need a full-sized bus, although we might not yet fill it completely (Austin, 2013).
4. The journals *European Economic History Review* and *Economic History of Developing Regions* are also important and influential, but because of their stated geographical focus they are not included in this bibliometric exercise.
5. Perfectly corresponding with economic growth data for the continent; see Jerven (2015).
6. The "reversal of fortunes" hypothesis was also the basis for a review article by Gareth Austin (2008). Austin's article engages the work of Nunn (2008) and Acemoğlu et al. (2001, 2002) directly, while Hopkins was discussing a wider range of "new" literature. A lively debate between Hopkins, Fenske, and me ensued in the journal *Economic History of Developing Regions* (Fenske 2010b, 2011; Jerven 2011a; Hopkins 2011).
7. This means that the bias toward the zero findings defense is misplaced as an answer to a critique by an economic historian who points out that the observations in a dataset are misleading or meaningless. The bias toward zero findings says that if the data are noisy, that should bias the results toward not finding support for a hypothesis. However, this disregards the fact that every usage of a bad dataset, whether it finds

results or not, tends to reinforce the authority of the descriptive levels or rankings in the misleading dataset.

8. Van de Walle (2007) dates the first to Cameroon in 1979.
9. The clearest statement was made by Rodney (1972) and Amin (1972).
10. One clear illustration of this debate found in the Kenya debate, as summarized in Leys (1996).
11. For a critique, see Leys (1996).
12. The first versions of the Penn World Table were published in the 1970s (Kravis et al., 1978), but the mainstream use of this dataset is dated to the 5.0 version, which was published in 1991 (Summers and Heston 1991).
13. Wheeler (1984) could be considered an early forerunner in this debate.
14. For a review of the growth evidence, see Jerven (2011b) and Jerven (2015).
15. The exclusion restriction in the instrumental variable regression of Acemoğlu et al. 2001 is that the mortality rates of European settlers more than 100 years ago have no effect on GDP per capita today other than through institutional development.

2 Seeing Like an African State in the Twentieth Century

1. For a review of the studies up and until 1987 see Manning 1987, and for a summary of some of the more recent research see Jerven et al. 2012.
2. Indeed, sometimes country data are made up before the countries exist. See, for instance, the controversy on settler mortality data in the debate between Albouy (2012) and Acemoğlu et al. (2001).
3. Data as of July 25, 2019. Aske Bonde (2012) collected part of the data for an honors thesis I supervised at Simon Fraser University. My research assistant Rolf Åsmund Hansen subsequently updated the data at the Norwegian University of Life Sciences.
4. Algeria, Benin, Botswana, Burkina Faso, Cape Verde, Côte d'Ivoire, Egypt, Eswatini, Gabon, Gambia, Kenya, Lesotho, Malawi, Mali, Mauritania, Mauritius, Mozambique, Morocco, Namibia, Rwanda, São Tomé and Príncipe, Senegal, Seychelles, South Africa, Tanzania, Tunisia, Uganda, Zambia, and Zimbabwe.
5. The World Bank, Living Standards Measurement Survey, https://surveys.worldbank.org/lsms.
6. Although some efforts have been made in this regard; see Bowden et al. (2008).
7. UN-WIDER is the United Nations University World Institute for Development Economics Research.
8. "Afrobarometer is [a] non-partisan, pan-African research institution conducting public attitude surveys on democracy, governance, the

economy and society in 30+ countries repeated on a regular cycle." "About Us," Afrobarometer, www.afrobarometer.org/about.

9. Population figures for the preceding two paragraphs were calculated using 2016 population figures available from the United Nations Department of Economic and Social Affairs, Population Division, World Population Prospects 2019, January 13, 2016, https://esa.un.org /unpd/wpp/DataQuery.

3 New Data and New Perspectives on Economic Growth in Africa

1. The Maddison project has since updated the database, but as of yet it has not incorporated recent attempts to provide new historical national accounts for African countries in the colonial period (Maddison, 2018).

2. For a review of early national accounting in Africa, see Ady (1963).

3. For country case studies on Botswana, Tanzania and Kenya consult Jerven 2010a, 2011d, 2011e.

4. For specific details on the calculation, see Prados de la Escosura (2012).

5. The term "level estimate" refers here to estimating GDP per capita in local or international dollars as opposed to growth estimates, which measure percentage annual change in production or income.

6. The World Bank database provides GDP estimates based on national account files estimates for most countries back to 1960. The Maddison dataset and Penn World Table have been extended back to 1950 for some countries.

7. See papers deriving from the project "Historical Patterns of Development and Underdevelopment: Origins and Persistence of the Great Divergence" at the Centre for Economic Policy Research, https://cordis.europa.eu/pro ject/id/225342.

8. Present-day names of these countries.

9. We know more about West Africa than other parts of Africa, we know less about regional trade than world trade, and we know more about the Atlantic trade than the Indian Ocean trade.

10. According to Williamson (2011: 29), "the best measure of the terms of trade is the ratio of a weighted average of export and imported prices quoted in local markets, including home import duties, that captures the impact of relative prices on the local market" where the "the weights of course, should be constructed from the country in question."

11. See Austin (2008) for a review of this literature and for a reformulation of a factor endowment perspective for sub-Saharan Africa. More

specifically, Tosh (1980) emphasizes the negative impact on food production in the savannah, Hill (1970) stresses the importance of capital investment and entrepreneurship in the production of cocoa, and Smith (1976) highlighted the deindustrialization of textile production in Nigeria.

12. For a review, see Cooper (1993). In particular, Arrighi (1970) criticized the use of the Lewis model to explain the proletarization of the peasantry in Rhodesia. He argued that in that country, the state actively undermined peasant production by demanding taxes and alienating land.

13. There were two significant discrepancies. According to Kilby (1969), the market would have justified a start-up of cement and textile production as early as 1920 and the 1890s, respectively, but the country did not have factories in those industries until 1957.

14. The method used to calculate cocoa production assumed a constant relationship between cocoa output and capital formation, where output is a function of past labor used in planting. This method also assumes a constant per acre yield and uses prevailing daily wages from the blue book. It was assumed that it takes 170 labor days to bring an acre to the bearing age and that each acre bears 420 pounds of cocoa.

15. There is sometimes information missing from the underlying sources. In these instances, we interpolate if the gaps are relatively short.

16. See Table 3.26 in the Appendix for a breakdown of the price indices.

4 State Capacity across the Twentieth Century: Evidence from Taxation

1. These are of course overlapping and vary from territory to territory.

2. We have some information about types and rates of taxation in well-studied precolonial centralized states that may well be used for country studies, such as the work on the Sokoto Caliphate (Jumare, 1998). A recent promising study of the Merina Kingdom in present-day Madagascar should be noted (Sanchez, 2019). A number of centralized kingdoms collected taxes in a mix of kind, tribute, and cash; for a review, see Goody (1969).

3. Some studies that focus on a single country or on one part of one country do not publish data in a fashion that is accessible to other researchers.

4. Cogneau et al., (2018) would argue that French colonies moved from direct taxation to trade and more 'modern' taxation.

5. In cases where they have exactly the same spelling, we classified them only once and the algorithm applied the classification to all countries that had the item "licenses for businesses" or its exact translation.

6. In cases where it is not possible to differentiate licenses into either category, we assumed that they were equally distributed among direct and indirect taxes. However, it is important to note that the category of unclassifiable licenses constitutes an extremely small share of all licenses.

7. This pattern remains robust even given two important caveats to the interpretation of the data in the early colonial period. First, the growth is from a low base and is hard to pinpoint when the taxes colonial authorities collected were simply replacing unrecorded taxes collected in precolonial Africa. Second, in some areas, forced labor was important as a *de facto* substitute for taxes (van Waijenburg, 2018). Again, this would bias observed growth upward if one does not observe the growth attributable to taxation moving from labor in kind to payment in cash. Unfortunately, exact magnitudes are hard to pin down given that colonial states did not keep systematic records of these practices, which were coming under increased international scrutiny even at the time. We calculated the potential bias from this effect, largely drawing on the estimates calculated by van Waijenburg (2018). While it is not negligible, it is not consequential for our overall assessment of growth.

8. As can be seen in Figure 4.2, much of the revenue growth during this period is due to "other ordinary" revenue, which consist of fees, licenses, and receipts from the rapidly expanding state enterprises such as railways.

9. Our data indicates that African polities received increasing amounts of metropolitan subsidies during the wars that are not captured in these figures, as they are counted as extraordinary revenue. These subsidies could add as much as 25 percent to revenue during the wars.

10. Colonial authorities introduced export taxes in this period, often through marketing boards for cash crops.

11. This matches the pattern Cage and Gadenne (2017) describe.

5   Wages and Poverty: From Roots of Poverty to Trajectories of Living Standards

1. In Jane Guyer's keynote address titled "Paupers. Percentiles. Precarity. Analytics for poverty studies in Africa," at the conference "The history of poverty in Africa: A central question?" at Columbia University on March 6, 2014, she reminded us of the need to historicize poverty. She explained that her first field work took her from northern England to northern Nigeria and remarked that at that time it was not necessarily

evident that she was traveling from a situation of affluence to a situation of extreme poverty.

2. How this positive change in formal economies through wages and labor participation should be interpreted, in particular in the context of so-called dual economies, has been the subject of fierce debate.

3. Manning does refer to the work of Berry (1975), which uses oral sources to trace development in West Africa during the cocoa boom.

4. But there are also datasets and archives that could have been used and were not, as I argue in Jerven (2011a).

5. And in particular, if economists had not focused so much on the shortfall in average growth in Africa and focused more on temporal change; see Jerven (2015).

6. And more, it is an interdisciplinary effort; see Harriss (2002).

7. Space does not permit a full review of the lessons from other historical scholarship on poverty in Africa.

8. It is fair to say that this is the mainstream scholarly interpretation of poverty outside the field of economics. This interpretation of course owes a great deal to Amartya Sen's cross-disciplinary work in economics and philosophy.

9. $1.90 a day as of October 1, 2015.

10. There is little way of guaranteeing the provenance of these price data.

11. For a fuller review of poverty measurement problems, see Jerven (2016b).

12. It is then assumed that an average family of two adults and two to three children would require three of these consumption baskets, the equivalent of a household subsistence basket.

13. De Zwart (2013) follows the same methodology in his calculation of real wages in Cape Colony (present-day South Africa) from its founding in 1652 to unification in 1910. Rönnbäck (2014) uses trade company books to calculate wages in precolonial Ghana.

14. Bolt and Hillbom (2016) is an early publication on a project that is creating social tables to investigate the relative trends in different wage earners in colonial Africa.

Bibliography

Primary Sources

Government Documents

Colony of the Gambia. 1932. *Report and Summary of the Census of the Gambia*. Bathurst: The Government Printer.

Government of Nigeria. 1933. *Census of Nigeria, 1931*. London: The Crown Agents for the Colonies.

Kenya Colony and Protectorate. 1932. *Report on the Census Enumeration of the Non-Native Population Made in the Colony and Protectorate of Kenya on the Night of the 6th March, 1931*. Nairobi: The Government Printer.

Nyasaland Protectorate. 1932. *Report on the Census of 1931*. Zomba: The Government Printer.

Sierra Leone. 1931. *Report of Census for the Year 1931*. Freetown: The Government Printer.

Tanganyika Territory. 1932 *Report on the Non-Native Census Taken in the Territory on the Night of the 26th April, 1931*. Dar es Salaam: The Government Printer.

Uganda Protectorate. 1933. *Census Returns, 1931*. Entebbe: The Government Printer.

Databases

Afrobarometer. Accessed November 18, 2015. https://afrobarometer.org.

Demographic and Health Surveys, USAID. The DHS Program, available datasets. Accessed November 13, 2015. www.dhsprogram.com/data/available-datasets.cfm.

Maddison, Angus. 2018. Maddison Project Database 2018. Gronigen Growth and Development Center. www.rug.nl/ggdc/historicaldevelopment/maddison/releases/maddison-project-database-2018.

United Nations Department of Economic and Social Affairs. 2004. *Population to 2300*. New York: United Nations.

United Nations Department of Economic and Social Affairs, World Population and Housing Census Programme. 2010. Census dates for all countries. https://unstats.un.org

World Bank. 2015. PovcalNet. Accessed October 29, 2015. http://iresearch.worldbank.org/PovcalNet.

Secondary Sources

Aboagye, P. Y., and J. Bolt. 2018. Economic inequality in Ghana, 1891–1960. African Economic History Working Paper Series no. 38.

Acemoğlu, D., and S. Johnson. 2005. Unbundling institutions. *Journal of Political Economy*, 113 (5): 949–995.

Acemoğlu, D., S.H. Johnson, and J.A. Robinson. 2001. The colonial origins of comparative development: An empirical investigation. *American Economic Review*, 91 (5): 1369–1401.

2002. Reversal of fortune: Geography and institutions in the making of the modern world income distribution. *Quarterly Journal of Economics*, 117 (4): 1231–1294.

Acemoğlu, D., and J.A. Robinson. 2010. Why is Africa poor? *Economic History of Developing Regions*, 25: 21–50.

2012. *Why Nations Fail: The Origins of Power, Prosperity, and Poverty.* New York: Random House/Crown.

Ady, P.H. 1963. Uses of national accounts in Africa. In L.H. Samuels, ed., *African Studies in Income and Wealth*. London: Bowes & Bowes, 52–65.

Ahlerup, P., T. Baskaran, and A. Bigsten. 2014. Tax innovations and public revenues in sub-Saharan Africa. *Journal of Development Studies*, 51 (6): 689–706.

Akpalu, W., G. Agenyo, E.M. Letete, and M. Sarr. 2017. Evolution of institutions in Ghana and implications for economic growth. ERSA working paper 710. Economic Research Southern Africa, Cape Town.

Akram-Lodhi, A.H. 1988. Review of *The Development of Capitalism in Africa* by John Sender and Sheila Smith. *Review of African Political Economy*, 41: 97–102.

Albers, T., M. Jerven, and M. Suesse. 2019. Taxation, fiscal capacity and economic development in Africa, c.1890–c.2015: Lessons from a new dataset. Paper presented at the conference Understanding State Capacity, University of Manchester, November 28 and 29.

2020. The fiscal state in Africa: Evidence from a century of growth. African Economic History Working Paper Series No. 55. www.aehnetwork.org/working-papers/the-fiscal-state-in-africa-evidence-from-a-century-of-growth.

Albouy, D. 2012. The colonial origins of comparative development: An empirical investigation: Comment. *American Economic Review*, 102 (6): 3059–3076.

Alesina, A.F., W. Easterly, and J. Matuszeski. 2006. Artificial states. NBER working paper no. 12328. Cambridge, MA: National Bureau of Economic Research.

Alexopoulou, K. 2018. An anatomy of colonial states and fiscal regimes in Portuguese Africa: Long-term transformations in Angola and Mozambique, 1850s–1970s. PhD thesis, Wageningen University, the Netherlands.

Allen, R.C. 1999. Tracking the agricultural revolution in England. *Economic History Review*, 52 (2): 209–235.

   2000. Economic structure and agricultural productivity in Europe, 1300–1800. *European Review of Economic History*, 4 (1): 1–25.

   2009. *The British Industrial Revolution in Global Perspective*. Cambridge: Cambridge University Press.

Alsan, M. 2015. The effect of the tsetse fly on African development. *American Economic Review*, 105 (1): 382–410.

Álvarez-Nogal, C., and L. Prados de la Escosura. 2013. The rise and fall of Spain (1270–1850). *Economic History Review*, 66 (1): 1–37.

Amin, S. 1972. Underdevelopment and dependence in black Africa: Origins and contemporary forms. *Journal of Modern African Studies*, 10 (4): 503–524.

Andersson, J. 2017. Long-term dynamics of the state in Francophone West Africa: Fiscal capacity pathways 1850–2010. *Economic History of Developing Regions*, 32 (1): 37–70.

   2018. *State Capacity and Development in Francophone West Africa*. Lund: Media-Tryck, Lund University.

Andersson, F., and J. Lennard. 2019. Irish GDP between the famine and the First World War: Estimates based on a dynamic factor model. *European Review of Economic History*, 23 (1): 50–71.

Annales. 2016. The economics of contemporary Africa. *Annales: Histoire, Sciences Sociales*, 71 (4): 504–505.

Arrighi, G. 1970. Labour supplies in historical perspective: A study of the proletarianization of the African peasantry in Rhodesia. *Journal of Development Studies*, 6: 197–234.

   2002. The African crisis: World systemic and regional aspects. *New Left Review*, 15: 5–36.

Artadi, E., and X. Sala-i-Martín. 2003. The economic tragedy of the XXth century: Growth in Africa. NBER working paper no. 9865. Cambridge, MA: National Bureau of Economic Research.

Ashraf, Q.H., and O. Galor. 2011. The 'Out of Africa' hypothesis, human genetic diversity, and comparative economic development. CEPR Discussion Paper No. DP8500.

Assenova, V.A., and M. Regele. 2017. Revisiting the effect of colonial institutions on comparative economic development. *PLoS ONE*, 12 (5): e0177100.

Austen, R. 1987. *African Economic History: Internal Development and External Dependency*. London: James Currey.

Austin, G. 2008. The 'Reversal of Fortune' thesis and the compression of history: Perspectives from African and comparative economic history. *Journal of International Development*, 20 (8): 996–1027.

2009. Poverty and development in sub-Saharan Africa, c.1450–c.1900: Reflections on the development of the economic historiography. Paper presented at the annual meeting of the European Historical Economics Society, Geneva, September 4.

2013. Where is 'here' anyway, and where should we be going? Promise and problems in the resurgence of African economic history. Fage lecture. University of Birmingham, August 5. www.birmingham.ac.uk/schools/historycultures/departments/dasa/news/2013/fage.aspx.

2014. Vent for surplus or productivity breakthrough? The Ghanaian cocoa take-off, c. 1890–1936. *Economic History Review*, 67 (4): 1035–1064.

Austin, G., J. Baten, and A. Moradi. 2007. Exploring the evolution of living standards in Ghana, 1880–2000: An anthropometric approach. Paper presented at the annual meeting of the Economic History Society, Exeter.

Austin, G., J. Baten, and B. van Leeuwen. 2012. The biological standard of living in early nineteenth-century West Africa: New anthropometric evidence for northern Ghana and Burkina Faso. *Economic History Review*, 65 (4): 1280–1302.

Austin, G., and S. Broadberry. 2014. Introduction: The renaissance of African economic history. *Economic History Review*, 67 (4): 893–906.

Austin, G., E.H.P. Frankema, and M. Jerven. 2017. Patterns of manufacturing growth in sub-Saharan Africa: From colonization to the present. In K. H. O'Rourke and J.G. Williamson, eds., *The Spread of Modern Industry to the Periphery since 1871*. Oxford: Oxford University Press, 345–374.

Barro, R.J. 1991. Economic growth in a cross section of countries. *Quarterly Journal of Economics*, 106 (2): 407–443.

Baskaran, T., and A. Bigsten. 2012. Fiscal capacity and the quality of government in sub-Saharan Africa. *World Development*, 45: 92–107.

Bates, R. 1981. *Markets and States in Tropical Africa: The political basis of agricultural policies*. Berkeley and Los Angeles: University of California Press.

Bates, R.H., G. Fayad, and A. Hoeffler. 2012. The state of democracy in sub-Saharan Africa. *International Area Studies Review*, 15 (4): 323–338.

Beegle, K.G., L. Christiaensen, A.L. Dabalen, and I. Gaddis. 2016. *Poverty in a Rising Africa*. Washington, DC: World Bank.

Berry, S. 1975. *Cocoa, Custom, and Socio-economic Change in Rural Western Nigeria*. Oxford: Clarendon Press, 1975.

Bertocchi, G., and F. Canova. 2002. Did colonization matter for growth? An empirical exploration into the historical causes of Africa's underdevelopment. *European Economic Review*, 46 (10): 1851–1871.

Besley, T., and T. Persson. 2014. Why do developing countries tax so little? *Journal of Economic Perspectives*, 28 (4): 99–120.

Besley, T., and M. Reynal-Querol. 2014. The legacy of historical conflict: Evidence from Africa. *American Political Science Review*, 108 (2): 319–336.

Bezemer, D., J. Bolt, and R. Lensink. 2014. Slavery, statehood, and economic development in sub-Saharan Africa. *World Development*, 57: 148–163.

Bhorat, H., R. Kanbur, and B. Stanwix. 2017. Minimum wages in sub-Saharan Africa: A primer. *World Bank Research Observer*, 32 (1): 21–74.

Bigsten, A. 1986. Welfare and economic growth in Kenya, 1914–76. *World Development*, 14 (9): 1151–1160.

Bird, R.M., and E.M. Zolt. 2005. Redistribution via taxation: The limited role of the personal income tax in developing countries. *Annals of Economics and Finance*, 15 (2): 625–683.

Block, S.A., K.E. Ferree, and S. Singh. 2003. Multiparty competition, founding elections and political business cycles in Africa. *Journal of African Economies*, 12 (3): 444–468.

Bloom, D.E., J.D. Sachs, P. Collier, and C. Udry. 1998. Geography, demography, and economic growth in Africa. *Brookings Papers on Economic Activity*, 2: 207–296.

Bockstette, V., A. Chanda, and L. Putterman. 2002. States and markets: The advantage of an early start. *Journal of Economic Growth*, 7 (4): 347–369.

Bolt, J., and D. Bezemer. 2009. Understanding long-run African growth: Colonial institutions or colonial education? *Journal of Development Studies*, 45 (1): 24–54.

Bolt, J., and E. Hillbom. 2016. Long-term trends in economic inequality: Lessons from colonial Botswana, 1921–74. *Economic History Review*, 69 (4): 1255–1284.

Bonde, A.N. 2012. Rapidly growing yet scantily known. Honours thesis, Simon Fraser University.

Bonnecase, V. 2009. Avoir faim en Afrique occidentale française: Investigations et représentations coloniales (1920–1960). *Revue d'Histoire des Sciences Humaines*, 21 (2): 151–174.

2015. Généalogie d'une évidence statistique: De la «réussite économique» du colonialisme tardif à la 'faillite' des États africains (v.1930–v.1980). *Revue d'histoire moderne et contemporaine*, 4 (62–66): 33–63.

Bourguignon, F., and C. Morrisson. 2002. Inequality among world citizens: 1820–1992. *American Economic Review*, 92 (4): 727–744.

Bowden, S., B. Chiripanhura, and P. Mosley. 2008. Measuring and explaining poverty in six African countries: A long period approach. *Journal of International Development*, 20 (8): 1049–1079.

Broadberry, S., B.M.S. Campbell, A. Klein, M. Overton, and B. van Leeuwen. 2015. *British Economic Growth, 1270–1870*. Cambridge: Cambridge University Press.

Broadberry, S., H. Guan, and D.D. Li. 2018. China, Europe, and the great divergence: A study in historical national accounting, 980–1850. *Journal of Economic History*, 78 (4): 955–1000.

Burnside, C., and D. Dollar. 1997. Aid, policies, and growth. World Bank Policy Research working paper no. 569252. Policy Research Department, World Bank. https://papers.ssrn.com/sol3/papers.cfm?abstract_id=569252.

Burnside, C., and D. Dollar. 2000. Aid, policies, and growth. *American Economic Review*, 90 (4): 847–868.

Bush, B., and J. Maltby. 2004. Taxation in West Africa: Transforming the colonial subject into the "governable person." *Critical Perspectives in Accounting*, 15 (1): 5–34.

Cage, J., and L. Gadenne. 2017. Tax revenues, development, and the fiscal cost of trade liberalization, 1792–2006. CEPR Discussion Paper no. DP12469. https://papers.ssrn.com/sol3/papers.cfm?abstract_id=3082295.

Carr-Hill, R. 2016. Measuring development progress in Africa: The denominator problem. In M. Jerven and D. Johnston, eds., *Statistical Tragedy in Africa? Evaluating the database for African economic development*. Abingdon: Routledge, 136–154.

Chambers, R. 1997. *Whose Reality Counts? Putting the First Last*. London: Intermediate Technology Publications.

Cogneau, D. 2003. Colonisation, school and development in Africa: An empirical analysis. Document de travail DT/2003/01. Université Paris-Dauphine, Développement, Institutions et Mondialisation.

2016a. The economic history of Africa: Renaissance or dawn? *Annales: Histoire, Sciences Sociales*, 71 (4): 539–556.

2016b. History, data and economics for Africa: Can we get them less wrong? Reply to Morten Jerven's "Trapped between tragedies and miracles: Misunderstanding African economic growth." *Development Policy Review*, 34 (6): 895–899.

Cogneau, D., and Y. Dupraz. 2014. Questionable inference on the power of pre-colonial institutions in Africa. Unpublished paper. HAL Archives-Ouvertes. https://halshs.archives-ouvertes.fr/halshs-01018548/document.

2015. Institutions historiques et développement économique en Afrique: Une revue sélective et critique de travaux récents. *Histoire & mesure*, 30 (1): 103–134.

Cogneau, D., Y. Dupraz, and S. Mesplé-Somps. 2018. Fiscal capacity and dualism in colonial states: The French empire 1830–1962. PSE Working Papers no. 2018–27. HAL Archives-Ouvertes. https://hal.archives-ouvertes.fr/halshs-01818700v3/document.

Collier, P. 2007. *The Bottom Billion: Why the Poorest Countries Are Failing and What Can Be Done about It*. New York: Oxford University Press.

Collier, P., and J.W. Gunning. 1999a. Explaining African economic performance. *Journal of Economic Literature*, 37 (1): 64–111.

Collier, P., and J.W. Gunning. 1999b. Why has Africa grown slowly? *Journal of Economic Perspectives*, 13 (3): 3–22.

Comin, D., W. Easterly, and E. Gong. 2010. Was the wealth of nations determined in 1000 BC? *American Economic Journal: Macroeconomics*, 2 (3): 65–97.

Cooper, F. 1993. Africa and the world economy. In F. Cooper, A. Isaacman, F. Mallon, W. Roseberry, and S.J. Stern, eds., *Confronting Historical Paradigms: Peasants, Labor, and the Capitalist World System in Africa and Latin America*. Madison: University of Wisconsin Press, 84–203.

Curtin, P.D. 1975. *Economic Change in Precolonial Africa: Senegambia in the Era of the Slave Trade*. Madison: University of Wisconsin Press.

Deane, P. 1953. *Colonial Social Accounting*. New York: Cambridge University Press.

Deaton, A. 2010. Instruments, randomization, and learning about development. *Journal of Economic Literature*, 48 (2): 424–455.

Deaton, A., and A. Heston. 2010. Understanding PPPs and PPP-based national accounts. *American Economic Journal: Macroeconomics*, 2 (4): 1–35.

Desrosières, A. 1998. *The Politics of Large Numbers: A History of Statistical Reasoning*. Cambridge, MA: Harvard University Press.

De Zwart, P. 2013. Real wages at the Cape of Good Hope: A long-term perspective, 1652–1912. *Tijdschrift Voor Sociale en Economische Geschiedenis*, 10 (2): 28–58.

Di John, J. 2009. Taxation, governance and resource mobilisation in sub-Saharan Africa: A survey of key issues. Real Instituto Elcano working paper 49/2009. Royal Elcano Institute, Madrid.

Domschke, E., and D.S. Goyer. 1986. *The Handbook of National Population Censuses: Africa and Asia.* Westport: Greenwood Press.

Durlauf, S.N., P.A. Johnson, and J.R.W. Temple. 2005. Growth econometrics. In P. Aghion and S. Durlauf, eds., *Handbook of Economic Growth.* Amsterdam: Elsevier, 555–667.

Easterly, W. 2001. The lost decades: Explaining developing countries' stagnation in spite of policy reform 1980–1998. *Journal of Economic Growth*, 6 (2): 135–157.

Easterly, W., M. Kremer, L. Pritchett, and L.H. Summers. 1993. Good policy or good luck? Country growth performance and temporary shocks. *Journal of Monetary Economics*, 32 (3): 459–483.

Easterly, W., and R. Levine. 1997. Africa's growth tragedy: Policies and ethnic divisions. *Quarterly Journal of Economics*, 112 (4): 1203–1250.

Englebert, P. 2000a. Pre-colonial institutions, post-colonial states, and economic development in tropical Africa. *Political Research Quarterly*, 53 (1): 7–36.

2000b. Solving the mystery of the Africa dummy. *World Development*, 28 (10): 1821–1835.

Ewald, J.J. 1992. Slavery in Africa and the slave trades from Africa. *The American Historical Review*, 97 (2): 465–485.

Fariss, C.J., T. Anders, F.J. Linder, C.D. Crabtree, Z.M. Jones, and J. N. Markowitz. 2017. Latent estimation of GDP, GDP per capita, and population from historic and contemporary sources. Unpublished paper. https://arxiv.org/pdf/1706.01099.pdf

Feinstein, C.H. 1972. *National Income, Expenditure and Output of the United Kingdom, 1855–1965.* Cambridge: Cambridge University Press.

Fenske, J. 2010a. The causal history of Africa: A response to Hopkins. MPRC Paper no. 24458. Munich Personal RePEc Archive. https://mpra .ub.uni-muenchen.de/24458/2/MPRA_paper_24458.pdf.

2010b. The causal history of Africa: A response to Hopkins. *Economic History of Developing Regions*, 25 (2): 177–212.

2011. The causal history of Africa: Replies to Jerven and Hopkins. *Economic History of Developing Regions*, 26 (2): 125–131.

Fetter, B. 1987. Decoding and interpreting African census data: Vital evidence from an unsavory witness. *Cahiers d'etudes africaines*, 27 (105): 83–105.

Fogel, R.W., and G.R. Elton. 1983. *Which Road to the Past? Two Views of History.* New Haven, CT: Yale University Press.

Fourie, J., and J.L. van Zanden. 2013. GDP in the Dutch Cape Colony: The national accounts of a slave-based society. *South African Journal of Economics*, 81 (4): 467–490.

Frankel, J.A., and D.H. Romer. 1999. Does trade cause growth? *American Economic Review*, 89 (3): 379–399.

Frankema, E. 2010. Raising revenue in the British empire, 1870–1940: How 'extractive' were colonial taxes? *Journal of Global History*, 5 (3): 447–477.

2011. Colonial taxation and government spending in British Africa, 1880–1940: Maximizing revenue or minimizing effort? *Explorations in Economic History*, 48 (1): 136–149.

Frankema, E., and M. Jerven. 2012. The missing link: Reconstructing African population growth, 1850–present. Paper presented at the African Studies Association UK Conference, Leeds, September 6–8.

2014. Writing history backwards or sideways: Towards a consensus on African population, 1850–2010. *Economic History Review*, 67 (4): 907–931.

Frankema, E., and M. van Waijenburg. 2011. African real wages in Asian perspective, 1880–1940. Working Paper no. 2. Centre for Global Economic History, Utrecht University.

2012. Structural impediments to African growth? New evidence from real wages in British Africa, 1880–1965. *Journal of Economic History*, 72 (4): 895–926.

2014. Metropolitan blueprints of colonial taxation? Lessons from fiscal capacity building in British and French Africa, c. 1880–1940. *Journal of African History*, 55 (3): 371–400.

2018. Africa rising? A historical perspective. *African Affairs*, 117 (469): 543–568.

Gallup, J., and J. Sachs. 2001. The economic burden of malaria. In J. G. Breman, A. Egan, and G.T. Keusch, eds., *The Intolerable Burden of Malaria: A New Look at the Numbers*. Supplement, *American Journal of Tropical Medicine and Hygiene*, 64: 85–96.

Gardner, L. 2010. Decentralization and corruption in historical perspective: Evidence from tax collection in British Colonial Africa. *Economic History of Developing Regions*, 25 (2): 213–236.

2012. *Taxing Colonial Africa: The Political Economy of British Imperialism*. Oxford: Oxford University Press.

Goody, J. 1969. Economy and feudalism in Africa. *Economic History Review*, 2nd series, 22 (3): 393–405.

Green, E. 2012. On the size and shape of African States. *International Studies Quarterly*, 56 (2): 229–244.

Greyling, L., and G. Verhoef. 2017. Savings and economic growth: A historical analysis of the Cape Colony economy, 1850–1909. *Economic History of Developing Regions*, 32 (2): 127–176.

Grier, R.M. 1999. Colonial legacies and economic growth. *Public Choice*, 98 (3/4): 317–335.

Harari, Y.N. 2014. *Sapiens: A Brief History of Humankind*. London: Vintage Books.

Harriss, J. 2002. The case for cross-disciplinary approaches in international development. *World Development*, 30 (3): 487–496.

Havik, P.J. 2012. Colonial administration, public accounts and fiscal extraction: Policies and revenues in Portuguese Africa (1900–1960). *African Economic History*, 41: 159–221.

    2015. *Administration and Taxation in Former Portuguese Africa: 1900–1945*. Newcastle upon Tyne: Cambridge Scholars Publishing.

Herbst, J. 2000. *States and Power in Africa: Comparative Lessons in Authority and Control*. Princeton, NJ: Princeton University Press.

Hill, P. 1970. *Studies in Rural Capitalism in West Africa*. Cambridge: Cambridge University Press.

Hogendorn, J. and Gemery, H. 1988. Continuity in West African monetary history? An outline of monetary development. *African Economic History*, 17: 127–146.

Hogendorn, J. and Johnson, M. 1986. *The Shell Money of the Slave Trade*. Cambridge: Cambridge University Press.

Hopkins, A.G. 1973. *An Economic History of West Africa*. London: Longman.

    1986. The World Bank in Africa: Historical reflections on the African present. *World Development*, 14 (12): 1473–1487.

    1987. Big business in African studies. *Journal of African History*, 28 (1): 119–140.

    2009. The new economic history of Africa. *Journal of African History*, 50 (2): 155–177.

    2011. Causes and confusions in African history. *Economic History of Developing Regions*, 26 (2): 107–110.

    2020. *An Economic History of West Africa*. 2nd ed. New York: Routledge.

Iliffe, J. 1987. *The African Poor: A History*. New York: Cambridge University Press.

Inikori, J.E. 1981. Market structure and the profits of the British African trade in the late eighteenth century. *Journal of Economic History*, 41 (4): 745–776.

Isham, J., L. Pritchett, M. Woolcock, and G. Busby. 2005. The varieties of resource experience: Natural resource export structures and the political economy of economic growth. *World Bank Economic Review*, 19: 141–174.

Jedwab, R., F. Meier zu Selhausen, and A. Moradi. 2018. The economics of missionary expansion: Evidence from Africa and implications for development. CSAE Working Paper Series 2018–07, Centre for the Study of African Economies, University of Oxford.

Jenkins, R. 2006. Where development meets history. *Commonwealth & Comparative Politics*, 44 (1): 2–15.

Jerven, M. 2010a. Accounting for the African growth miracle: The official evidence, Botswana 1965–1995. *Journal of Southern African Studies*, 36 (1): 73–94.

2010b. African growth recurring: An economic history perspective on African growth episodes, 1690–2010. *Economic History of Developing Regions*, 25 (2): 127–154.

2010c. The relativity of poverty and income: How reliable are African economic statistics? *African Affairs*, 109 (434): 77–96.

2011a. A clash of disciplines? Economists and historians approaching the African past. *Economic History of Developing Regions*, 26 (2): 111–124.

2011b. The quest for the African dummy: Explaining African post-colonial economic performance revisited. *Journal of International Development*, 23 (2): 288–307.

2011c. Users and producers of African income: Measuring African progress. *African Affairs*, 110 (439): 169–190.

2011d. Growth, stagnation or retrogression? On the accuracy of economic observations, Tanzania, 1961–2001. *Journal of African Economies*, 20 (3): 377–394.

2011e. Revisiting the consensus on Kenyan economic growth, 1964–1995. *Journal of Eastern African Studies*, 5 (1): 2–23.

2012. An uneven playing field: National income estimates and reciprocal comparison in global economic history. *Journal of Global History*, 7: 107–128.

2013. *Poor Numbers: How We Are Misled by African Development Statistics and What to Do about It*. Ithaca, NY: Cornell University Press.

2014a. *Economic Growth and Measurement Reconsidered in Botswana, Kenya, Tanzania, and Zambia, 1965–1995*. Oxford: Oxford University Press.

2014b. A West African experiment: Constructing a GDP series for colonial Ghana, 1891–1950. *Economic History Review*, 67 (4): 964–992.

2015. *Africa: Why Economists Got It Wrong*. London: Zed Books.

2016a. Data and statistics at the IMF: Quality assurances for low-income countries. Background Paper BP/16/6. IMF Independent Evaluation Office, Washington, DC.

2016b. Development by numbers: A primer. DRI working paper. Development Research Institute, New York University.

2016c. The failure of economists to explain growth in African economies. *Development Policy Review*, 34 (6): 889–893.

2017. How much will a data revolution in development cost? *Forum for Development Studies*, 44 (1): 31–50.

2018a. Controversy, facts and assumptions: Lessons from estimating long term growth in Nigeria, 1900–2007. *African Economic History*, 46 (1): 104–136.

2018b. The history of African poverty by numbers: Evidence and vantage points. *The Journal of African History*, 59 (3): 449–461.

Jerven, M., G. Austin, E. Green, C. Uche, E. Frankema, J. Fourie, J.E. Inikori, A. Moradi, and E. Hillbom. 2012. Moving forward in African economic history: Bridging the gap between methods and sources. AEHN working paper no. 1. African Economic History Network.

Johnson, M. 1970. The Cowrie currencies of West Africa. Part I. *The Journal of African History*, 11 (1): 17–49.

Jones, P., 2013. History matters: New evidence on the long run impact of colonial rule on institutions. *Journal of Comparative Economics*, 41 (1): 181–200.

Jumare, I.M. 1998. Colonial taxation in the capital emirate of Northern Nigeria. *African Economic History*, 26: 83–97.

Keen, M., and M. Mansour. 2010. Revenue mobilisation in sub-Saharan Africa: Challenges from globalisation. I – Trade Reform. *Development Policy Review*, 28 (5): 553–571.

Kelly, M. 2019. The standard errors of persistence. UCD Centre for Economic Research Working Paper Series no. WP 19/13. UCD School of Economics, University College Dublin.

Kenny, C., and D. Williams. 2001. What do we know about economic growth? Or, why don't we know very much? *World Development*, 29 (1): 1–21.

Kilby, P. 1969. *Industrialization in an Open Economy: Nigeria 1945–1966.* Cambridge: Cambridge University Press.

Kirk-Greene, A.H.M. 1980. The thin white line: The size of the British colonial service in Africa. *African Affairs*, 79 (314): 25–44.

Kravis, I.B., A.W. Heston, and R. Summers. 1978. Real GDP per capita for more than one hundred countries. *Economic Journal*, 88 (350): 215–242.

Kremer, M. 2003. Randomized evaluations of educational programs in developing countries: Some lessons. *American Economic Review*, 93 (2): 103–106.

Kuczynski, R.R. 1937. *Colonial Population.* London: Oxford University Press.

1948. *Demographic Survey of the British Colonial Empire. Vol. 1: West Africa.* Oxford: Oxford University Press.

La Porta, R., F. Lopez-de-Silanes, and A. Shleifer. 2008. The economic consequences of legal origins. *Journal of Economic Literature*, 46 (2): 285–332.

La Porta, R., F. Lopez-de-Silanes, A. Shleifer, and R. Vishny. 1999. The quality of government. *Journal of Law, Economics, and Organization*, 15 (1): 222–279.

Labrousse, A. 2016. Poor numbers: Statistical chains and the political economy of numbers. *Annales: Histoire, Sciences Sociales*, 71 (4): 507–538.

Law, R. 1992. Posthumous questions for Karl Polanyi: Price inflation in pre-colonial Dahomey. *The Journal of African History*, 33 (3): 387–420.

Lee, M.M., and N. Zhang. 2013. The art of counting the governed: Census accuracy, civil war, and state presence. CDDRL Working Papers 146. Center on Democracy, Development and the Rule of Law, Stanford University.

Leys, C. 1996. *The Rise and Fall of Development Theory*. Nairobi: EAEP.

Maddison, A. 2009. Historical statistics of the world economy: 1–2006 AD. Accessed June 10, 2018. www.ggdc.net/maddison/.

Malanima, P. 2011. The long decline of a leading economy: GDP in central and northern Italy, 1300–1913. *European Review of Economic History*, 15 (2): 169–219.

Manning, P. 1975. Review of *An Economic History of Nigeria, 1860–1960* by R. Olufemi Ekundare. *The International Journal of African Historical Studies*, 8 (2): 314–317.

1983. Contours of slavery and social change in Africa. *American Historical Review*, 88 (4): 835–857.

1987. The prospects for African economic history: Is today included in the long run? *African Studies Review*, 30 (2): 49–62.

2010. African Population: Projections, 1851–1961. In K. Ittmann, D.D. Cordell, and G. Maddox, eds., *The Demographics of Empire: The Colonial Order and the Creation of Knowledge*. Athens, OH: Ohio University Press, 245–275.

Mansour, M. 2014. A tax revenue dataset for sub-Saharan Africa: 1980–2010. FERDI working paper I19. Fondation pour les Études et Recherches sur le Développement International, Clermont-Ferrand, France.

Maslin, M. 2004. *Global Warming: A Very Short Introduction*. New York: Oxford University Press.

Mauro, P. 1995. Corruption and growth. *Quarterly Journal of Economics*, 110 (3): 681–712.

Mazumdar, D., with A. Mazaheri. 2000. Wages and employment in Africa. Regional Program on Enterprise Development Paper #109.

McEvedy, C., and R. Jones. 1978. *Atlas of World Population History*. Harmondsworth: Penguin.

Michalopoulos, S., and E. Papaioannou. 2010. Divide and rule or the rule of the divided? Evidence from Africa. Unpublished paper. https://ssrn.com/abstract=1696195.

2013. Pre-colonial ethnic institutions and contemporary African development. *Econometrica*, 81: 113–152.

2016. The long-run effects of the scramble for Africa. *American Economic Review*, 106 (7): 1802–1848.

2019. Historical legacies and African development. VoxDev, Accessed August 10, 2019. https://voxdev.org/topic/institutions-political-economy/historical-legacies-and-african-development.

Miers, S. and Roberts, R.L. eds. 1988. *The End of Slavery in Africa.* Madison: University of Wisconsin Press.

Mkandawire, T. 2010. On tax efforts and colonial heritage in Africa. *Journal of Development Studies*, 46 (10): 1647–1669.

Moradi, A. 2008. Confronting colonial legacies: Lessons from human development in Ghana and Kenya, 1880–2000. *Journal of International Development*, 20 (8): 1107–1121.

2009. Towards an objective account of nutrition and health in colonial Kenya: A study of stature in African army recruits and civilians, 1880–1980. *Journal of Economic History*, 69 (3): 719–754.

Mosley, P. 1963. *The Settler Economies: Studies in the economic history of Kenya and Southern Rhodesia 1900–1963.* Cambridge: Cambridge University Press.

Munro, J.F. 1976. *Africa and the International Economy, 1800–1960.* Totowa, NJ: Rowman and Littlefield.

Narayan, D., R. Patel, K. Schafft, A. Rademacher, and S. Koch-Schulte. 2000. *Voices of the Poor: Can Anyone Hear Us?* New York: Oxford University Press for the World Bank.

North, D.C. 1990. *Institutions, Institutional Change and Economic Performance.* Cambridge: Cambridge University Press.

Nunn, N. 2008. The long-term effects of Africa's slave trades. *Quarterly Journal of Economics*, 123 (1): 139–176.

2009. The importance of history for economic development. *Annual Review of Economics*, 1 (1): 65–92.

Nunn, N., and D. Puga. 2012. Ruggedness: The blessing of bad geography in Africa. *Review of Economics and Statistics*, 94 (1): 20–36.

Nunn, N., and L. Wantchekon. 2011. The slave trade and the origins of mistrust in Africa. *American Economic Review*, 101 (7): 3221–3252.

Okigbo, P. 1962. Nigerian national accounts, 1950–7. *Review of Income and Wealth* 1: 285–306.

Olsson, O. 2004. Unbundling ex-colonies: A comment on Acemoğlu, Johnson, and Robinson, 2001. Working Papers in Economics 146. Department of Economics, University of Gothenburg.

Organization for Economic Cooperation and Development. 2013. *African Economic Outlook 2013.* Paris: OECD.

Parker, J., and R. Rathbone. 2007. *African History: A Very Short Introduction*. Oxford: Oxford University Press.

Pinfold, J.R. 1985. *African Population Census Reports: A Bibliography and Checklist*. Munich: Hans Zell Publishers.

Population Research Center, University of Texas. 1965. *International Population Census Bibliography: Africa*. Austin: Bureau of Business Research, University of Texas.

Population Research Center, University of Texas. 1968. *International Population Census Bibliography: Supplement 1968*. Austin: Bureau of Business Research, University of Texas.

Porter, T.M. 1996. *Trust in Numbers: The Pursuit of Objectivity in Science and Public Life*. Princeton, NJ: Princeton University Press.

Posner, D.N. 2004. Measuring ethnic fractionalization in Africa. *American Journal of Political Science*, 48 (4): 849–863.

Prados de la Escosura, L. 2012. Output per head in pre-independence Africa: Quantitative conjectures. *Economic History of Developing Regions*, 27 (2): 1–36.

Price, G.N. 2003. Economic growth in a cross-section of nonindustrial countries: Does colonial heritage matter for Africa? *Review of Development Economics*, 7 (3): 478–495.

Prichard, W. 2016. Reassessing tax and development research: A new dataset, new findings, and lessons for research. *World Development*, 80: 48–60.

Prichard, W., A. Cobham, and A. Goodall. 2016. The ICTD government revenue dataset. ICTD Working Paper 19. International Centre for Tax and Development, Brighton, UK.

Prichard, W., and D.K. Leonard. 2010. Does reliance on tax revenue build state capacity in sub-Saharan Africa? *International Review of Administrative Sciences*, 74 (6): 653–675.

Pritchett, L. 1998. Patterns of economic growth: Hills, plateaus, mountains, and plains. World Bank Policy Research Working Paper 1947. World Bank, Washington, DC.

Ray, D. 2010. Uneven growth: A framework for research in development economics. *Journal of Economic Perspectives*, 24 (3): 45–60.

Reid, R. 2011. Past and presentism: The "precolonial" and the foreshortening of African history. *The Journal of African History*, 52 (2): 135–155.

Richens, P. 2009. The economic legacies of the "thin white line": Indirect rule and the comparative development of sub-Saharan Africa. Economic History Working Papers 131/09. Department of Economic History, London School of Economics and Political Science.

Rodney, W. 1972. *How Europe Underdeveloped Africa*. London: Bogle-L'Ouverture Publications.

Rönnbäck, K. 2014. Living standards on the pre-colonial Gold Coast: A quantitative estimate of African laborers' welfare ratios. *European Review of Economic History*, 18 (2): 185–202.

Sachs, J.D. 2003. Institutions don't rule: Direct effects of geography on per capita income. NBER Working Paper no. 9490. National Bureau of Economic Research, Cambridge, MA.

Sachs, J.D., and A. Warner. 1995. Economic reform and the process of global integration. *Brookings Papers on Economic Activity*, 1: 1–118.

1997. Sources of slow growth in African economies. *Journal of African Economies* 6: 335–376.

Sala-i-Martín, X., and M. Pinkovskiy. 2010. African poverty is falling ... much faster than you think! NBER Working Paper no. 15775. National Bureau for Economic Research, Cambridge, MA.

Samuel, B. 2016. Studying Africa's large numbers. *Annales: Histoire, Sciences Sociales*, 71 (4): 557–579.

Sanchez, S.F. 2019. La valeur du "bain royal" (fandroana): Échanges tributaires et souveraineté dans le Royaume de Madagascar au xixe siècle. *Revue d'histoire du XIXe siècle*, 59: 71–94.

Schön, L., and O. Krantz. 2012. The Swedish economy in the early modern period: Constructing historical national accounts. *European Review of Economic History*, 16 (4): 529–549.

Scott, J.C. 1998. *Seeing Like a State: How Certain Schemes to Improve the Human Condition Have Failed*. New Haven, CT: Yale University Press.

Seers, D. 1976. The political economy of national accounting. In A. Caincross and M. Puri, eds., *Employment, Income Distribution and Development Strategy: Problems of the Developing Countries*. New York: Holmes & Meier Publishers., 193–209.

Serajuddin, U., H. Uematsu, C. Wieser, N. Yoshida, and A. Dabalen. 2015. Data deprivation: Another deprivation to end. World Bank Policy Research working paper WPS7252. Policy Global Practice Group and Development Data Group, World Bank.

Serra, G. 2014. An uneven statistical topography: The political economy of household budget surveys in late colonial Ghana, 1951–1957. *Canadian Journal of Development Studies*, 35 (1): 9–27.

2018. "Hail the census night": Trust and political imagination in the 1960 population census of Ghana. *Comparative Studies in Society and History*, 60 (3): 659–687.

Simelane, S.E. 2002. The population of South Africa: An overall and demographic description of the South African population based on census 1996. Occasional paper 2002/01. Statistics South Africa, Pretoria.

Smith, S. 1976. An extension of the vent-for-surplus model in relation to long-run structural change in Nigeria. *Oxford Economic Papers*, new series, 28 (3): 426–446.

Smits, J.-P., P. Woltjer, and D. Ma. 2009. A dataset on comparative historical national accounts, ca. 1870–1950: A time-series perspective. GGDC Working Papers GD-107. Groningen Growth and Development Centre, University of Groningen.

Stephens, R. 2013. *A History of African Motherhood: The Case of Uganda, 700–1900*. Cambridge: Cambridge University Press.

Stern, N. 1989. The economics of development: A survey. *The Economic Journal*, 99 (397): 597–685.

Stolper, W.F. 2014. *Planning without Facts*. Cambridge, MA: Harvard University Press.

Summers, R., and A. Heston. 1991. The Penn World Table (Mark 5), an expanded set of international comparisons, 1950–1988. *Quarterly Journal of Economics*, 106 (2): 327–368.

Szereszewski, R. 1965. *Structural Changes in the Economy of Ghana, 1891–1911*. London: Weidenfeld and Nicolson.

Tabutin, D., and B. Schoumaker. 2004. The demography of sub-Saharan Africa from the 1950s to the 2000s: A survey of changes and a statistical assessment. *Population* (English Edition, 2002–), 59 (3–4): 457–519; 522–555.

Tavares, J., and R. Wacziarg. 2001. How democracy affects growth. *European Economic Review*, 45 (8): 1341–1378.

Taylor, A.M., and M.P. Taylor. 2004. The purchasing power parity debate. *Journal of Economic Perspectives*, 18 (4): 135–158.

Temple, J. 2016. Morten Jerven, and what economists do and don't get wrong. *Development Policy Review*, 34 (6): 901–905.

Tertilt, M. 2005. Polygyny, fertility, and savings. *Journal of Political Economy*, 113 (6): 1341–1370.

The Economist. 2015. We happy few: Nigeria's population has been systematically exaggerated. Special Report. *The Economist*, June 18. www.economist.com/special-report/2015/06/18/we-happy-few.

Thornton, J. 1977. Demography and history in the Kingdom of Kongo, 1550–1750. *Journal of African History*, 18 (4): 507–530.

Tosh, J. 1980. The cash-crop revolution in tropical Africa: An agricultural appraisal. *African Affairs*, 79 (314): 79–94.

Toye, J.F.J., and R. Toye. 2003. The origins and interpretation of the Prebisch-Singer thesis. *History of Political Economy*, 35 (3): 437–467.

United Nations Statistics Division. 2015. 2010 World Population and Housing Census Programme. September 18. Accessed November 2,

2015. https://archive.unescwa.org/2010-world-population-and-housing-census-programme.

Van de Walle, E. 1968. The availability of demographic data by regions in tropical Africa. In J.J.C. Caldwell and C. Okonjo, eds., *The Population of Tropical Africa*. London: Longman, 28–33.

Van de Walle, N. 2007. *African Economies and the Politics of Permanent Crisis*. Cambridge: Cambridge University Press.

Van Leeuwen, B., J. van Leeuwen-Li, and P. Foldvari. 2012. *Education as a Driver of Income Inequality in Twentieth-Century Africa*. Munich Personal RePEc Archive, https://mpra.ub.uni-muenchen.de/43574/.

Van Waijenburg, M. 2018. Financing the African colonial state: The revenue imperative and forced labor. *Journal of Economic History*, 78 (1): 40–80.

Van Zanden, J.L., and B. van Leeuwen. 2012. Persistent but not consistent: The growth of national income in Holland 1347–1807. *Explorations in Economic History*, 49 (2): 119–130.

Vansina, J. 1982. Towards a history of lost corners in the world. *Economic History Review*, new series, 35 (2): 165–178.

1986. Knowledge and perceptions of the African past. In B. Jewsiewicki and D. Newbury, eds., *African Historiographies: What History for which Africa?* Beverly Hills, CA: Sage, 28–42.

Vollrath, D. 2016. Evolving research on growth and development. *Development Policy Review*, 34 (6): 907–910.

Wallerstein, I. 1979. *The Capitalist World-Economy*. Cambridge: Cambridge University Press.

Ward, M. 2004. *Quantifying the World: UN Ideas and Statistics*. Bloomington: Indiana University Press.

Wheeler, D. 1984. Sources of stagnation in sub-Saharan Africa. *World Development*, 12 (1): 1–23.

Williamson, J.G. 2011. *Trade and Poverty: When the Third World Fell Behind*. Cambridge, MA: MIT Press.

World Bank. 1981. *Accelerated Development in Sub-Saharan Africa: An Agenda for Action*. Washington, DC: World Bank.

World Bank. n.d. International Comparison Program (ICP). www.worldbank.org/en/programs/icp.

Wrigley, C. 1982. Population and history: Some innumerate reflexions. In C. Fyfe and D. McMaster, eds., *African Historical Demography. Vol. II: Proceedings of a Seminar Held in the Centre of African Studies, University of Edinburgh, 24th and 25th April 1981*. Edinburgh: Centre of African Studies, University of Edinburgh, 17–31.

Young, C. 1994. *The African Colonial State in Comparative Perspective*. New Haven, CT: Yale University Press.

Index